*Handel: Water Music and Music for the Royal Fireworks*

This handbook covers Handel's best-known public music, the *Water Music*, written at the outset of his English career, and the *Music for the Royal Fireworks*, the last and largest of his orchestral creations. The genesis of these two orchestral suites is examined in its political as well as musical context; practical questions of performance style and inter-pretation are balanced by an enquiry into Handel's compositional processes, and the relationship of his other large-scale orchestral compositions, especially the *Concerti a due cori*, to these suites. Original source material is set alongside the most recent theories on Handel's character and working methods. In particular the problem of 'borrowings' is addressed with reference to most recent identifications of Handel's sources, together with the later presentation of these works in the nineteenth and twentieth centuries, with an account of recordings, editions and a summary of performance questions.

Founder and director of The Academy of Ancient Music since 1973, CHRISTOPHER HOGWOOD continues to work internationally with both period-instrument and modern ensembles, and has more than 200 critically acclaimed recordings to his name. He is currently engaged with editing keyboard music from the Fitzwilliam Museum for *Musica Britannica*, the complete keyboard works of Henry Purcell for the Purcell Society, Mendelssohn's seven great concert overtures for Bärenreiter and the original version of *La Revue de Cuisine* by Martinů, recently recorded by the Czech Philharmonic (Supraphon). His many publications include a survey of patronage through the ages (*Music at Court*), biographical studies of Haydn, Mozart and Handel, a history of the trio sonata, and *Music in Eighteenth-Century England* (Cambridge, 1983). Hogwood's academic positions include Honorary Professor of Music at the University of Cambridge, Fellowships at Jesus and Pembroke Colleges, Cambridge, and Visiting Professor at the Royal Academy of Music. He also teaches regularly at Harvard University.

# CAMBRIDGE MUSIC HANDBOOKS

GENERAL EDITOR  Julian Rushton

*Recent titles*

# Handel: *Water Music* and *Music for the Royal Fireworks*

## Christopher Hogwood

*Honorary Professor of Music*
*University of Cambridge*

CAMBRIDGE UNIVERSITY PRESS
Cambridge, New York, Melbourne, Madrid, Cape Town, Singapore, São Paulo

CAMBRIDGE UNIVERSITY PRESS
The Edinburgh Building, Cambridge CB2 2RU, UK
Published in the United States of America by Cambridge University Press, New York

www.cambridge.org
Information on this title: www.cambridge.org/9780521544863

First published 2005

Printed in the United Kingdom at the University Press, Cambridge

*A catalogue record for this book is available from the British Library*

ISBN-13 978-0-521-83636-4 hardback
ISBN-10 0-521-83636-0 hardback
ISBN-13 978-0-521-54486-3 paperback
ISBN-10 0-521-54486-6 paperback

# *Contents*

# Illustrations

# *Preface*

For ease rather than accuracy, *Water Music* and *Music for the Royal Fireworks* are conventionally packaged as the 'alpha and omega' of Handel's orchestral music, marking off a composing lifetime devoted to opera, oratorio and the orchestra. They were, as intended, popular from the first and have never lagged since, and for that reason are sometimes taken, quite wrongly, as being the epitome of his style; but they are far from being typical of Handel.

The composer would have been surprised – even (judging by warnings from his contemporaries) irritated – at the prospect of being remembered for such occasional pieces rather than his prime love, dramatic vocal music. True, a statue was erected to him during his lifetime in Vauxhall Gardens, that focus of liberal entertainment where *le bon ton* consorted with the less respectable. But he shared this honour with Homer and Milton, serious, epic artists (all three eventually blind) and it is a more significant pointer to his place in the artistic order that Handel was valued in his own lifetime as 'the more than Homer of his Age'.[1]

There would be other reasons for Handel's surprise at the present-day status of these instrumental pieces. Despite the ease of technique on display in them, Handel was very little interested in orchestral music *per se*, nor was he ever very stimulated by the suite as a formal construction apart from its balletic implications. On the whole his orchestral music was provoked either by the demands of publication or as an attempt to attract more public to his oratorios with virtuoso add-ons. There is no evidence that he ever attended a concert of purely instrumental music and, apart from the freak creation of *Water Music*,

[1]  William Cowper, *The Task*, VI, 647 (1785)

he would never have known any entertainment of more than twenty minutes' length that was not basically vocal. Handel did not 'do' instrumental concerts: all his orchestral music, organ concertos and concerti grossi were planned as additions to his vocal entertainments. The two exceptions, *Water Music* and *Music for the Royal Fireworks* (WM and FM) were politically generated, occasional in every sense and peripheral to Handel's main goals.

In spite of thirty-two years between them, the two suites display surprising similarities: ease of melodic invention, instrumental colouring, organised 'alternativo' scorings for repeats, formal control, and the 'friendly' use of royal and military sounds. Both were played by 'super-orchestras'. Apart from the forces mustered for *La Resurrezione* in Rome (1708) and state occasions (royal funerals, coronations), Handel's normal expectations for an opera or oratorio orchestra were moderate; but when offered larger resources, he instinctively knew how to employ them for maximum impression and utmost variety.

In both works Handel shows himself a congenital borrower, but also a consummate craftsman. *Water Music* and *Fireworks Music* stand at either end of a long and well-travelled composing life, from escape via Hamburg to Italy as 'il caro Sassone' to residence in London as 'the great and good Mr Handel'. It is worth exploring not only what Handel as a composer discovered in the course of this life, but also what we must rediscover today to make the most of his legacy. As modern listeners and performers (amateur or professional) we want to know more about Handel's methods of composing, and the problems and choices he leaves to the present-day performer. We are also intrigued to see what aspects of Handel's technique and vision changed during his lifetime, and what mannerisms of style and method remained constant. A glimpse into his working methods is promised by his life-long preference for making generous use of pre-existing materials and the evidence of his working scores. There is no autograph version of *Water Music*, but the score of *Fireworks Music* carries the advantages (and disadvantages) of having been worked over several times by the composer.

Handel's accommodations to social and political pressures are fascinating, if less clearly documented than the subtle shifts and re-scoring of his compositions. Although firmly established outside the frontiers of court life, he was an enlightened monarchist and proud of his position as an artistic bridge between King and people at moments of celebration. Handel rarely failed to respond to the demands of national and political theatre and fitted into British history as neatly as his music has since come to define British sensibility.

## *Credits and thanks*

The British Library (Chris Banks, Nicolas Bell, David Way),
The British Museum (Sheila O'Connell, Department of Prints
and Drawings), City of Westminster Archives Centre (Hilary
Davies), The Fitzwilliam Museum, Cambridge (Stella
Panayatova), The British Library Sound Archive (Timothy
Day, Jonathan Summers), The Royal Society of Musicians of
Great Britain (Maggie Gibb, Oliver Davies), The Foundling
Museum, Gerald Coke Handel Collection (Katharine Hogg),
The Royal Artillery Museum (Royal Arsenal, Woolwich),
Henry Watson Music Library, Manchester (Ros Edwards),
Donald Burrows, Anthony Hicks, Terence Best, John Roberts,
David Hunter, David Way, Stephen Rose, Johannes Gebauer,
David Greer, James Brooks Kuykendall, Jan Smaczny,
Elizabeth Fleming, David Vickers, Pierre-François Goy,
Rosemary Moravec-Hilmar, Heather Jarman, Simon Shaw,
David Scrase, Milo Keynes, Jacob Simon, David Lasocki,
William Gudger, Robert Darnton, Michael Dodds, Thomas
Drescher, Teri Noel Towe, William Wroth, Anthony Halstead,
Jonathan Freeman-Attwood, Richard Gooder, Crispian
Steele-Perkins, Mark Argent and Guillermo Brachetta

# Editions and abbreviations

Much of the detailed description in this handbook will be more lucid with a modern score alongside the reader. Several editions are available, of varying accuracy and cost, and the most relevant are referred to by the following abbreviations:

*Chrysander*            *G. F. Händel's Werke: Ausgabe der Deutschen Händelgesellschaft*, vol. 47 (*Water Music, Fireworks Music*, the three *Concerti a due cori* and the two *Concerti* associated with *Fireworks Music*), 1886. Reprinted in full by Gregg Press Incorporated, 1965, Lea Pocket Scores L.P.S. No. 139 and Kalmus Miniature Score Series, no. 1362. *Water Music* and *Fireworks Music* reissued in Dover Miniature Scores, 1999

*Fiske* WM              *The Water Music*, ed. Roger Fiske, Edition Eulenburg no. 1308, London, 1973

*Fiske* FM              *The Musick for the Royal Fireworks*, ed. Roger Fiske, Edition Eulenburg no. 1307, London, 1979

*Redlich* FM / WM       Hallische Händel-Ausgabe (Bärenreiter Urtext scores): *Wassermusik*, ed. Redlich, (1962), *Music for the Royal Fireworks*, ed. Redlich (1962). Revised editions by Terence Best and Christopher Hogwood in preparation

*Hudson*                Hallische Händel-Ausgabe (Bärenreiter Urtext scores): *Concerti a due cori*, ed. Hudson (1983)

HWV [Händel Werke Verzeichnis] numbers refer to Bernd Baselt, *G. F. Händel: Thematisch-systematisches Verzeichnis* (Leipzig and Kassel, 1978–86).

A facsimile of Handel's autograph manuscript containing *Fireworks Music* and the two Concertos HWV 335a and 335b, together with *A Description of the Machine for the Fireworks* and a selection of contemporary engravings, is published by Bärenreiter-Verlag, Kassel (2004). More specific references to manuscript and early printed sources for *Water Music* and *Fireworks Music* are listed in their respective chapters.

# 1

## *The character of the man*

> The Figure's odd; yet who wou'd think?
> (Within this Tunn of Meat & Drink)
> There dwells the Soul of soft Desires,
> And all that HARMONY inspires.

'I am myself alone' reads the Shakespearian inscription on a scroll decorating Goupy's caricature of Handel as a bewigged and well-dressed hog playing the organ, with the remnants of gluttony evident all around him (Plate 1). Joseph Goupy, painter and scene designer, was a close friend of Handel until (so Walpole tells us) this caricature and inscription created a rift – based on the 'evidence' that Goupy received no legacy in Handel's will; but many other close friends were not mentioned in that document. By the standards of eighteenth-century satire, the verses accompanying 'The Charming Brute' were both critical and complimentary; another, more exotic version reads:

> Strange Monsters have Adorn'd the Stage,
> Not Afric's Coast produces more,
> And yet no Land nor Clime nor Age,
> Have equal'd this Harmonious Boar.[1]

Maybe he was difficult, unusual, over-interested in food, independent, larger than life in all senses and short-tempered with it – but as a musician, the verses emphasise, he was unique and unrivalled. He was also private, and to many people, then as now, not easily explained; in spite of becoming a national monument, he was (and remains) an international enigma.

Handel's self-sufficiency had been noted for years. John Mainwaring in his *Memoirs of the Life of the Late George Frederic Handel*, a biography based on conversations with Handel's assistant, John Christopher Smith,

The Figure's odd . yet who wou'd think
Within this Tun of Meat and Drink.
There dwells the soul of soft Desires
And all that HARMONY inspires :

THE
Charming BRUTE

Can contrast such as this be found?
Upon the Globe's extensive Round;
There can — you Hogshead is his Seat
His sole Devotion is to Eat .

I AM MYSELF ALONE.

Plate 1  Engraving of a caricature by Joseph Goupy, 1754

describes the composer's unorthodox independence from his early days in
the Hamburg opera, comparing him to Pascal and Tycho Brahe for his
determination to follow his own choice of career. Setting out for Italy to
seek his fortune 'on his own bottom' he showed an egalitarian attitude to
patronage that meant he would never have to complain, as Bach did, that

'those in charge are odd and ambivalent towards music, which means I have to live with almost non-stop vexation, envy, and persecution'.[2] Handel was never liable to suffer at the death of a sole patron, nor be threatened with prison or an employer whose wife was 'amusa' or (like Haydn) with the dissolving of the cappella on the death of his princely patron. When Handel was offered a court position in Berlin, the argument went that 'if he once engag'd in the King's service, he must remain in it, whether he liked it, or not; that if he continued to please, it would be a reason for not parting with him; and that if he happened to displease, his ruin would be the certain consequence'. As a result, Handel never in his life took a 'tenured' position of the sort that Bach, Mozart or Haydn accepted; his was always a form of 'regulated employment' with a specific object and an end-plan in mind.

Handel was not the first German to decide that England offered the best prospects for a freelance musician at the beginning of the eighteenth century. Finger, Galliard, Keller, Greber and Pepusch had all preceded him, and the peripatetic Johann Sigismund Cousser (who had lived with Lully for six years and came to London in 1704) wrote out a series of rules for what a 'German' (in his case, Hungarian) might expect in coming to England, exchanging secure employment by a city or court for the more empirical world of public concerts and *ad hoc* patronage by the nobility.

Cousser offered a total of thirty-three rules for 'What a virtuoso should observe upon arriving in London', among them:

> Find good lodging.
> Retain your freedom and have it in the contract that you are permitted to perform outside the theatre whenever you wish.
> Be proud but greet everyone politely, for the English like to be flattered.
> Associate cordially with the musicians, but without great familiarity; seldom go drinking with them. If you wish to pay them special honour, do it in your own lodgings.
> Prepare yourself with music to fit their taste – no pathos certainly, and short, short recitatives.
> Praise the deceased Purcell to the skies and say there has never been the like of him.
> Make yourself acquainted with the best masters, such as Lullie [Loeillet], Pepusch, etc.
> Because of their great impertinence, don't engage an English servant.[3]

In letter or spirit, Handel followed the essence of these suggestions. He was proud and independent, secured lodgings on his own terms in such palaces as Cannons and Burlington House, struck up a close acquaintance with Pepusch, made due deference to elements of Purcell's style and the English taste, and employed a German man-servant. In addition he was a great composer.

Handel fitted into the society and system that he had adopted with ease, although he remained a private enigma in many respects. He left no account of his political feelings, but his allegiances can be seen in the long list of compositions for royal celebrations and the speed with which he could rally to the support of the royal PR machine when asked. He was openly accounted a royalist by society; conversely it amounted to *lèse-majesté* not to love Handel, according to Lord Hervey: 'an anti-Handelist was looked upon as an anti-courtier, and voting against the Court in Parliament was hardly a less remissible or more venial sin than speaking against Handel'.[4] He balanced his favours, courting the Prince of Wales as well as his father, and maintained connections with the opposite end of the political field. But in the end, as Donald Burrows points out, 'many of his strongest patrons and collaborators were, like Charles Jennens . . . supporters of the Old Succession (without necessarily being Jacobites)'.[5]

Several contemporary German commentators wrongly described Handel as the Capellmeister of the Court in London. Not only did Handel shrewdly avoid commitment,[6] but in fact George I was in no position to make such appointments. It was no longer within his purview to allocate funds either for a royal Director of Music or for the maintenance of an opera, as he had in Hanover; such expenses were now dealt with by Parliamentary decree, the purse strings tightly controlled by the young Robert Walpole, Chancellor of the Exchequer. Added to which, Handel was 'other', i.e. not British. The most the King could offer was a continuation of the 'retaining' pension conferred by Queen Anne, and a position as Music Master to the Princesses.

Handel's independence was thus guaranteed both from within and without; nor was he in any doubt of his worth, as the satirical press was aware: in *Harmony in an Uproar*, an anonymous 1734 pamphlet, 'Handel' describes his progress in the first person:

I was immediately admitted into the good Graces of the Court, and principal Grandees; who were all ravished with the Novelty and Exquisiteness of my Compositions: In consequence of which I was declar'd principal Composer to their O[per]as; and *should have enjoyed* the same Station in the Court Chapels and Publick Temples, only that Place could not be conferr'd upon a Foreigner: Yet upon all Solemn Occasions, they were obliged to have Recourse to me for their Religious Musick, tho' their ordinary Services were all compos'd and performed by Blockheads that were Natives; they claiming from several Laws a Right hereditary, to have their Places in their Temples supply'd with Fools of their own Country.

Handel's eventual naturalisation in 1727 made him eligible to write the anthems for the coronation of George II which set his style firmly in the public mind as 'sublime' and also 'voluminous' (there were said to be 160 instrumentalists employed in the coronation service). Dramatic musical creations with voices remained Handel's life-time obsession, and, like any man of the theatre, his work was for the most part driven by the demands of his audience; exceptions such as *Semele* or *Hercules* were risky gestures of independence. In this arena his life was determined by his public, not his patrons. Obstinacy *per se* is not an intrinsically admirable quality in an artist even when coupled with fine craftsmanship; it needs to be validated by association with a power base, community support, a feeling that here is a conviction that *should* be shared. Italian *opera seria* eventually failed for doctrinal as well as economic reasons: the power base of people who both believed and could afford the principles it exemplified became too rarefied and distracted by Enlightenment ideals. But out of this withdrawal of support there emerged a 'new' Handel, with music allied to the Bible and theories of a 'New Israel', speaking of patriotism, warfare and celebration (and also bourgeois entertainment), and a new success.

Almost as much can be said about Handel's ability to adapt as his inability to bend: independent fortitude was allied in his character with political and professional astuteness. In these terms, his career was not unique, but an early model for a new style of career as a freelance in a foreign country. Many of the questions that have been asked of Kurt Weill – another German expatriate transplanted to a different English-speaking country – could equally well be directed at Handel.[7] To what extent was Handel also 'a composer in search of coordinates'? Were his 'projects variously defined by collaborators'? Certainly many librettists, impresarios and politicians would have said so. In their attitude to the public, both composers followed a path that made audiences central to their aesthetic calculations in a way which might equally be described as openly 'commercial' or 'responsive, flexible, and inventive'. Handel stood by his principles as long as he (and his backers) possibly could. In the opera wars 'Mr Handel's efforts to call back the public taste' were admired until finally declared ineffectual: 'the house is deserted, the undertakers are ruined'. But like Weill, Handel was also 'a composer of circumstance; it was his strength and the key to his survival and success'. A change of attitude to 'the people' is observable in both composers during the course of their lives, shrewdly absorbed by Handel from English democracy in action and politically promoted by Weill's principal collaborator Brecht in the USA; and both showed a 'genuine connection with the multitude' in writing music that spoke to and for a contemporary public.

With outside pressures so dominant, one might question whether such careers could be continuous and consistent ('*konsequent*') and it is true that Handel's natural pattern of development is a balance of spurts followed by periods of consolidation and the repeating and refining of new discoveries; but he was far from being at the mercy of events. His constant awareness of his own past (his self-referential borrowings are only one signal) and his personal resilience make the positive and life-affirming music a direct portrayal of the man. He was, for this period, an example of the ideal modern composer – an 'articulate thinker, capable of seeing his art in the Enlightenment context', his work displaying 'a sense of self-awareness, responsibility and mature judgement of art conducted in the spirit of a scientific enquiry'.[8]

# 2

## Politics and power

While blest with thy Celestial Airs,
How vain we count the Views of life,
The Miser's Hopes, the Lover's Cares,
Domestic Feuds, and Public Strife!
(from *An Ode on Mr Handel, On his Playing on the Organ*, 1722, by Daniel Prat)

This feeble ode by the Revd Prat, 'formerly Chaplain to the King', was the first of several such eulogies wished on Handel in his lifetime. With equal incompetence, they all show that Handel was well on the way to becoming a national classic before he was even forty. His music and following had been noted in court circles as an ideal means to gratify the King and, when necessary, pacify the public – the well-known political technique of 'seduce and sedate'. 'Spin' had discovered its master of music, and the political manipulators, as well as the royal chaplain, had realised the emollient powers of such art against increasing 'Domestic Feuds' within the royal family, and 'Public Strife' in the wider political arena.

Handel was aloof: politically sensitive and at the same time capable of holding his own independent median position, whichever way the political wind was blowing. The biggest political jolt since his arrival in England had been the change of regime in August 1714, when the sudden death of Queen Anne put paid to the expectations of many Tory aristocrats. After confounding the 'knavish tricks' of the Jacobite rebellion of November 1715, George I looked for the security of a 'Whig supremacy' with no audible opposition. His succession had been carefully planned; representatives of the German court had been present in London for the last four years of the Queen's reign,[1] and Handel merely joined an existing colony, in theory working both in Hanover and London; he was described in the

English press as 'the famous Mr *Hendel*, a retainer to the Court of *Hanover*'. In fact, Handel had negotiated terms of engagement which left him free to travel and work outside the Hanoverian court ('he had leave to be absent for a twelve-month or more, if he chose it and to go whithersoever he pleased'),[2] and he appears to have been curtly dismissed in 1713. The reasons may not have been totally musical; mild espionage was a popular second job for travelling musicians in the seventeenth and eighteenth centuries. Handel was certainly used as a source of information on Queen Anne's state of health, and may have traded other items of inside knowledge as well. Was his spying perhaps not thorough enough? In any case the break was not as severe as legend suggests. From the Privy Papers we now know that Handel's royal pension (£200) from Queen Anne was continued under George, and the arrears eventually made good. He had even privately been given early reassurance that his position in England would be ratified when the House of Hanover took over, so the need for a public reconciliation with the monarch (the traditional fable associated with *Water Music*) did not really exist.

What was more at risk was King George's own popularity with his new people. The King found 'pageantry and splendour, badges and trappings of royalty' irksome and avoided public appearances whenever he could. There were also internal cracks; family disagreements between him and the Prince of Wales were becoming more open, so when the King left for Hanover in 1716, as he did each summer, he refused to leave his son with the full powers of regent, reducing him to 'Guardian of the Realm and Lieutenant'. The Prince and Princess eventually relocated to Leicester House, after their children had been confiscated by the King, and began to cultivate an alternative town society, giving parties and balls for the disaffected nobility. Princely support for Walpole and Townshend (pushed into opposition by a split amongst the Whigs) threatened the King's bold plan to make the Hanoverian succession the exclusive property of the Whig regime with only a nominal Tory opposition.

To counteract this division, ministers advised that the King needed to be seen by his people – at this period most people only knew the King's features from coinage or engravings, and fewer than 1 per cent of them had ever heard his voice. A royal progress was the traditional ritual of reassurance, and the least tiresome version, the summer water party, had been used with some frequency since 1715 to promote the royal family's appeal.[3]

A water spectacle enhanced by the music of Handel was more than just politically expedient, since George himself was a genuine Handelian. In addition to renewing his pension and employing him as Royal Music Master to the Princesses, the King, as Privy Papers from the Hanover archives show, was personally active in supporting Handel's operas: 'A man who attended *Admeto* 19 times in just over six weeks would seem to have been a genuine lover of Handel's music.'[4]

Given these facts, Mainwaring's account seems less convincing, but he may simply have been recording, via his conversations with J. C. Smith, the embellished memories of the composer himself:

> The King was persuaded to form a party on the water. HANDEL was apprised of the design, and advised to prepare some Music for that occasion. It was performed and conducted by himself, unknown to his Majesty, whose pleasure on hearing it was equal to his surprise. He was impatient to know whose it was, and how this entertainment came to be provided without his knowledge. The Baron then produced the delinquent . . .
> . . . HANDEL was restored to favour, and his Music honoured with the highest expressions of the royal approbation. As a token of it, the King was pleased to add a pension for life of 200 £ a year to that which Queen ANNE had before given him.[5]

Mainwaring appears to associate *Water Music* with the first year of the King's reign, without giving any further evidence; it is true that several such parties are documented, many instigated by the Prince and Princess of Wales, but none of the reports mentions Handel. The only such water event for which a connection with music by Handel is documented took place on 17 July 1717, and the descriptions in the press (and in more detail in diplomatic despatches) exactly match the scoring of what we now call *Water Music*. Parliament had just recessed, and a suitably lavish water progress was master-minded (and underwritten) by the King's brother-in-law, Baron Kielmansegge, after the leading impresario, John Heidegger (Swiss and never naturalised), had rather splendidly refused to be involved because it might prejudice his more commercial operations. Kielmansegge, Master of the Horse to George and a career diplomat, had married the King's illegitimate half-sister Sophie after previously being ambassador in Venice, where he had first 'taken great notice' of Handel in 1709. It was Kielmansegge who invited Handel to Hanover, where he was Capellmeister for more than two years, and Kielmansegge who was asked to break the news to Handel of his dismissal in 1713, so he clearly had a rapport with the young composer.

It was propitious timing for Handel. The fledgling opera company on which the composer had gambled had just closed its doors at the King's Theatre on 29 June; the musicians were unemployed and opera was not to re-open for three years. Apart from the 'reconstituted' Caroline *Te Deum*, no music had been commissioned from Handel by the Court since the death of Queen Anne and he had written nothing at all for the new monarch, already three years on the throne. Now was the moment for self-advertisement, as the aptly named *Daily Courant* (the world's first daily newspaper) reported (London, 19 July):

> On Wednesday Evening [17 July 1717], at about 8, the King took Water at Whitehall in an open Barge, wherein were also the Duchess of Bolton, the Duchess of Newcastle, the Countess of Godolphin, Madam Kilmanseck, and the Earl of Orkney. And went up the River towards Chelsea. Many other Barges with Persons of Quality attended, and so great a Number of Boats, that the whole River in a manner was cover'd a City Company's Barge was employ'd for the Musick, wherein were 50 Instruments of all sorts, who play'd all the Way from Lambeth (while the Barges drove with the Tide without Rowing, as far as Chelsea) the finest Symphonies, compos'd express for this Occasion, by Mr Hendel; which his Majesty liked so well, that he caus'd it to be plaid over three times in going and returning. At Eleven his Majesty went a-shoar at Chelsea, where a Supper was prepar'd, and then there was another very fine Consort of Music; which lasted till 2; after which, his Majesty came again into his Barge, and return'd the same Way, the Musick continuing to play till he landed.

The journey from what was sometimes called 'Whitehall Bridge' or 'Stairs' (see Plate 4, p. 75) (in fact a landing jetty) upriver to the rural hospitality of Chelsea would have been timed to coincide with the tidal flow. The Thames at this time was spanned by only one bridge (Westminster Bridge was not completed until 1746), and the narrow arches of the mediaeval London Bridge acted as sluice gates to hold the tidal pressures at bay. Precise timing by the watermen could ensure that both going and returning were with the tidal flow.[6]

The earliest royal barge from this time to survive is that of Frederick Prince of Wales, made in 1732 and now in the National Maritime Museum; it has special seats for two French horn players. However, the Hanover accounts detail the sizes of the vessels used in the *Water Music* party and the payments made from the Privy Purse to Jonathan Hill, Barge Master:[7]

*July ye 17<sup>th</sup> Carry'd his Majesty from Whitehall to Chelsea*

|  |  | £ | s |
|---|---|---|---|
| The Shallope | ... ... ... ... | 1. | 00. |
| The 12 Oar'd. Barge | ... ... ... ... | 1. | 00. |
| The 8 Oard. Barge | ... ... ... ... | 1. | 00. |
| The 6 Oard. Barge | ... ... ... ... | 0. | 10. |
|  |  | 3. | 10. |

The barge belonging to 'a City Company' transporting the musicians is more difficult to identify. It might have been the barge of the Weavers' Company, which was 72 feet long and needed eighteen rowers. For special occasions it was decorated with thirty small and two large pennants, a long streamer, banners of the Company and the City, and the King's Arms, with watermen in white linen waistcoats and the master and steersman in long coats of blue satin.[8] Even with a vessel of this size, the space required for fifty musicians (most of them standing) plus instruments and bowing room, not forgetting the oarsmen, the music-stands and the illumination needed for the return journey, must have created a scene more cramped than any opera pit, and decidedly less elegant than the later, carefully posed scenes of the Sharpe family's water party painted by Zoffany.

Naturally the King travelled in considerably greater comfort than the musicians, with only five members of the court in his barge. Four of them were ladies, but with impeccable military connections: the Duchess of Bolton, Henrietta Churchill, was daughter of the late Duke of Marlborough, the military hero, and the Countess of Godolphin was Marlborough's grand-daughter. One assumes that their husbands found places with the rest of the Court and other diplomats on the accompanying barges.

Friedrich Bonet, the Brandenburg Resident and one of Prussia's representatives in London, was in the party and sent his account in French to his masters in Berlin. He noted the anticipated absence of the Prince and Princess of Wales and also the unusual fact that this was an entertainment without singers:[9]

London, Friday 19th /30th July 1717[10]

A few weeks ago the King expressed to Baron Kilmanseck His desire to have a concert on the river, by subscription, similar to the masquerades this winter which the King never failed to attend. The Baron accordingly applied to Heidecker, – a Swiss by origin, but the cleverest purveyor of entertainments to the Nobility. The latter replied that, much as he would wish to comply with His Majesty's desires, he must reserve subscriptions for the great events, namely the masquerades, each of which brings him in 300 to 400 guineas net. Observing His Majesty's chagrin at these difficulties, M. de Kilmanseck undertook to provide the concert on the river at his own expense. The necessary orders were given and the entertainment took place the day before yesterday. About eight in the evening the King repaired to His barge, into which were admitted the Duchess of Bolton, Countess Godolphin, Mad. de Kilmanseck, Mad. Were and the Earl of Orkney, the Gentleman of the Bedchamber in Waiting. Next to the King's barge was that of the musicians, about 50 in number, who played on all kinds of instruments, to wit trumpets, horns, hautboys, bassoons, German flutes, French flutes, violins and basses; but there were no singers. The music had been composed specially by the famous Handel, a native of Halle, and principal composer of the King's Music. His Majesty approved of it so greatly that he caused it to be repeated three times in all, although each performance lasted an hour – namely twice before and once after supper. The evening [weather] was all that could be desired for the festivity, the number of barges and above all of boats filled with people desirous of participating was beyond counting. In order to make this entertainment the more exquisite, Madme. de Kilmanseck had arranged a choice supper in the late Lord Ranelagh's villa at Chelsea on the river, where the King went at one in the morning. He left at three o'clock and returned to St. James' about half past four. The concert cost Baron Kilmanseck £150 sterling for the musicians alone, but neither the Prince nor the Princess [of Wales] took any part in this festivity.[11]

Bonet's description matches exactly the instrumentation specified for *Water Music* in the form we now have it. For a total of fifty musicians we can extrapolate from the normal proportions of Handel's opera orchestra that there would probably have been six oboes, four bassoons, two trumpets, two horns and two 'flutes' doubling on *traversi* and recorders (possibly oboes as well), with an open-air string complement probably larger than his usual fourteen violins, five violas, four cellos and two double basses to bring the total up to fifty.[12] It is clear that multiple woodwinds were assumed for *Water Music*, and all surviving sources give 'Bassons' and 'Flauti Piccoli' in the plural. Wind-players frequently doubled; in some performing parts (see below, p. 22) the music for 'flutes' was actually included in the oboe parts. Handel was careful in his terminology: 'Flauto', 'German flute' or 'Common flute' was the treble recorder, 'Flauto piccolo' (sometimes 'fifth flute') the descant recorder, and 'Traverso' or 'French flute' the cross-flute as we know it.

The biggest sonic novelty of the evening would have been the stirring calls of the two *Cors de Chasse*. Four years earlier Mattheson had noted that in Germany 'the lovely, majestic hunting horns have now become very fashionable'.[13] Handel seems to have been a leader in the export of this sound; Mainwaring claims he was the first to use horns with voices in Italy (though there is no surviving music to prove this), following what he had learned in Hamburg from Keiser's example in *Octavia* (1705). Handel's players probably came from Bohemia or one of the German states, and would have played with their instruments raised in the air and the bells open ('pavillons en l'air' as most contemporary illustrations confirm); this was normal until, as Burney tells us in Rees's *Cyclopædia*, the Messing brothers arrived in England about 1740 and 'pretended to perform in all keys', that is, with hand-stopping.

Trumpets – the royal ingredient – were probably added at the last stage, and Handel may have adapted existing movements to take them. The *Water Music* commission was surely not 'Composed express for the Occasion' as the *Daily Courant* would have us believe; it would have been very unlike Handel to have resisted all recycling. After their first two showy movements, the trumpets are occupied exclusively with doubling, and in fact these movements are perfectly effective without them. There are also more identified borrowings in the trumpet movements than others, another hint of last-minute composition. Since it was rare for Handel to feature trumpets in two successive movements either in his opera or oratorio scores, their use helps us to decide on the original playing sequence (see below, p. 24).

There was surely no harpsichord on the barge, nor are timpani mentioned – both instruments unsuited to water – and the music is written to accommodate this fact. In WM11, for instance, the upper strings are used to provide the support for the trumpets that timpani might otherwise have given, and no final chords are left empty, without a third. Later, however, we find that indoor performances of the piece were often 'enhanced' with the addition of drum solos; Covent Garden advertised 'After the Play. Mr Handel's Water-Musick accompanied with French-Horns, Kettle-Drums, &c' (8 May 1736), reworded three days later to read 'After the Play. Mr Handel's Water-Musick, in which Mr Benj. Baker will beat the Kettle-Drums, accompanied with Trumpets and French-Horns'. A benefit performance in December 1748 for the bass Gustavus Waltz (said by both Burney and Hawkins to have been Handel's cook), concluded with 'the Water-Musick of Mr. Handel's, accompanied with Four Kettle-Drummers', headed by John Mitcheal Axt.

Mainwaring records that *Water Music* was 'performed and conducted by [Handel] himself', but neither he nor Bonet tells us whether he beat time or played the violin. There are no records of any specific players on the barge, but we know from earlier royal music parties that 'All, or most of the musicians at the Play-House in the Hay-Market [i.e. the opera house], are to be employ'd on this Occasion.' This was the *General Evening-Post* reporting on a 1716 water trip, which concluded, as usual, with supper and a ball. The opera orchestra at this date numbered about thirty-five players, so these were substantial entertainments. From this theatre connection we can surmise that one of Handel's players on the music barge was probably the trumpeter John Grano. His was a familiar face in the London music scene; he played in Handel's opera orchestra, gave music lessons, composed on demand, was familiar with 'Mr Smith the Opera Copyist' (Handel's assistant, John Christopher Smith) in the coffee houses and kept an entertaining and valuable diary of an ordinary musician's life in London during the first half of the eighteenth century. His wobbly career included an extraordinary period of several months when he was imprisoned in the Marshalsea for debt, and he records his frequently frustrated attempts to organise a benefit concert to raise money for his release. Even while a prisoner he appears to have been allowed outside for gainful employment, which included playing for water trips. In the absence of information from any of the other participants in the 1717 water trip, Grano's comments on similar, albeit smaller, events add colour otherwise missing from the *Water Music* story.

As we might expect, recruitment was by word of mouth: 'So to my Father's in Pall Mall, where I learnt that Mr Kytch the Hautboy was order'd to find me out to go on the Water to entertain the Royal Family the Day following' (26 August 1729).[14] Surprisingly, since the pay seems to have been generous, Grano turned the job down. A few months earlier, in his debtor's prison, he had been very grateful when 'a Young fellow belonging to the Guards came to me ... with a Guinea for my Performance on the Water last Monday' (31 May 1728).[15] Dr Johnson later claimed that a man could live 'with the appearance of gentility' in London on £30 a year.

On another occasion Grano received two guineas from a Mr Fleetwood for his services: – 'Got into the Barges by 8, went up the River, sounded pretty much, got above Chelsea ... [with] Anthony Cook the French Horn'. But even at such prices the music was less than fully appreciated: ''Twas about 9 at Night that we began to float back towards LONDON. The Music was hardly to be heard there was so great a Confusion.'[16]

Grano himself may have played in *Water Music* and he certainly later adapted several movements as trumpet duos for his two 'tawny' students while in Marshalsea Prison.[17] Since he also played flute and recorder, he could have been doubly useful on 'traverso' and 'flauto piccolo' as well as the trumpet.

Later performances of *Water Music* are documented, but without giving details of which portions were played: it is listed in 1722 at Stationers' Hall, and on 4 April that year Addison's play *The Drummer* was enhanced with 'select pieces of music ... with Trumpets, Flutes, German Flutes and French Horns, particularly Handel's *Water Musick*'. Since nothing was in print, the musicians must have played from manuscript parts, possibly loaned by the composer. It is conceivable that Handel actively refrained from having it published, the better to keep the use of it under his control. It eventually crept into print inaccurately and piecemeal; Walsh issued the overture only in 1725, and some minuet adaptations appeared in 1729. Walsh's fuller version (twelve numbers) appeared in 1733 in parts, but omitted everything requiring trumpets, which would have hindered sales; the resulting text is garbled and the sequence confused. Eventually in 1743 a version for harpsichord alone appeared, which included almost all the musical numbers. And this, surprising as it seems today, was all that existed in print for most of the eighteenth century, until Arnold's complete edition was published in 1788.

In fact, there were probably few opportunities for playing the entire sequence, even if it was seen as a single 'piece', and the published selections, inaccurate though they were, would have served as a convenient quarry for entertainment pieces.

*Water Music* appears not to have been played other than in extract form in the nineteenth century, which anyway preferred sacred and vocal Handel. When fuller suites were constructed in the 1920s (see Chapter 8), a small selection of numbers was made, usually ending with the D major hornpipe (WM12). Only when ensembles began to consider performing the whole sequence, as given in *Chrysander*, did theories of three separate suites emerge. Performances in the 1950s by Thurston Dart and Philomusica of London, and a recording made in 1959, used a revised edition based on the *Lennard* score, modified by reference to the *Walsh PP*, and offered a re-ordering of the movements into two 'large' suites and one 'chamber' suite.

# 3

# Water Music

When HANDEL deigns to strike the sense,
'Tis as when heaven, with hands divine,
Struck out the globe (a work immense!)
Where harmony meets with design.
> (*On Mr Handel's performance on the
> Organ ... by a Philharmonick*, printed
> in the Grub-Street Journal, 8 May 1735)

## Musical forms and formulas

Handel knew the aquatic *topos* well – the transformation of Acis into a fountain is a good example – but there is nothing identifiably watery in *Water Music*, unlike Vivaldi's *La tempesta di mare* or Telemann's programmatic 'Wasser Overture' *Hamburg Ebb and Flow*, where movements specifically depict mythological sea gods and goddesses, sailors dancing, and the ebb and flow of the tide in Hamburg harbour ('die Stille, das Wallen und die Unruhe des Wassers', 'der verliebte Neptunus', 'die lustigen Bots-Leut'). *Water Music* is, as literary analysts would say, *atopos*: 'unclassifiable' or 'of a ceaselessly unforeseen originality'.[1] Handel was writing pure entertainment music – music *on* the water rather than *about* water – and the same pieces had been or would be used for onshore masquerades and balls. In addition to his famous 'set pieces', Handel was regularly called on to compose entertainment and dance music; and it is not unreasonable to imagine such origins for many of the movements in *Water Music*. So should the resulting collection be approached as a random medley, an assemblage of separate suites or a planned and coherent whole?

Table 3.1 *Thematic index of Water Music*

Plate 2  Page of earliest manuscript score of *Water Music*, copied before 1719

## Sources and sequence

Our problems start with the fact that no autograph score of *Water Music* survives. This is unusual with Handel; the majority of his works exist in authoritative scores in his own hand, preserved in his own and the Royal libraries.[2] Manuscript parts of the component movements of *Water Music* may well have been lost to wind and weather, but the full score would not have been used in an eighteenth-century performance. Maybe it was a last-minute patchwork creation and no single score was compiled?

The earliest known manuscript score of the work was recently (October 2004) identified in the library of The Royal Society of Musicians of Great Britain, but a comprehensive study of this and a full *stemma* of the many secondary sources for *Water Music* are still awaited, as is a revised Urtext edition. Pending that, Table 3.1 (pp. 18–19) and the following summary give details of the major sources, and the sequence of movements in each.

## Manuscript sources

*RSM*: Library of The Royal Society of Musicians of Great Britain, London (no shelf mark). A full score untitled in the hand of two copyists: RM1, changing to Linike at fol. 40 (see Larsen),[3] and datable to before 1719, from the collection of Walter Hermann Laubach (not Lauterbach as given by Baselt in the HWV catalogue) who became a member of the RSM in 1893 and died in 1939. It contains unique interpolations in WM7 and confirms the proposed original sequence. See Plate 2.

*Sequence*: 1–22

*Malmesbury*: The Earl of Malmesbury's Collection, Hampshire Record Office, Winchester, 9 M 73/739; vol. 34, *Overtures and Miscellaneous Pieces*, pp. 139–70. A keyboard version of *Water Music* as '23 airs', copied by J. C. Smith, *c*. 1722 and formerly in the library of Elizabeth Legh. This source was not used for *Fiske*, although it would appear to indicate the original sequence.[4]

*Sequence*: 1–9, repeat of 3, 10–22

*Drexel*: New York Public Library, Drexel 5856. A keyboard version of *Water Music*, copied by J. C. Smith in the early 1720s, formerly in the library of Stafford Smith and possibly in the collection of Princess Amelia at Gunnersbury. Although headed *Overture for y$^e$ Water Music*, it contains no Overture but most of the other movements in the same sequence as *Malmesbury*.

*Sequence*: 5–9, 11–20, 22

*Aylesford*: Manchester Public Library, GB-Mp MS 130. Hd4. v. 354–368. Full score and parts from Charles Jennens' collection (score

1731–2, parts later 1740s), bought by Newman Flower. The oboe parts also contain the music for 'Travers' and 'Flautino'.

*Sequence*: 1–6, 8, 9, 7, 10–22

*Oxford*: Christ Church MSS 70–72 & 75. Four part-books (Violins I and II, Bassoon, Basso) in the hand of an unknown copyist, early 1730s. It gives a reduced version of nine movements, plus one from Op. 3.

*Sequence*: 6–9, [Menuet Op 3/4], 18–20, 13, 14, 22

*Lennard*: Cambridge, Fitzwilliam Museum MU MS 836, from the Barrett Lennard collection. Full score copied by J. C. Smith *c*. 1738; pp. 153–208 contain 'The Water Musick' omitting no. 10. This source was not known to *Chrysander*, but possibly used by Arnold; the extra movement listed by Smith[5] as following no. 16 does not exist. The bass is thoroughly figured in two movements only: no. 6 (bars 1–18 only) and no. 18.

*Sequence*: 1–9, 11, 12, 22, 16, 17, 13–15, 18–21

*Granville*: London, British Library, Egerton 2946. Full score copied (possibly from *Lennard*) by John Christopher Smith between 1736 and 1743. The MS belonged originally to Bernard Granville (1709–75), of Calwich Abbey, co. Stafford, a friend and supporter of Handel, and brother of Mrs Delaney.

*Sequence*: 1–12, 22, 16, 17, 13–15, 18–21

*Shaftesbury*: London, Foundling Museum, Gerald Coke Handel Collection, shelf-mark HC 486. Full score copied by Larsen's copyist S2, 1738–41.

*Sequence*: 1–12, 22, 13–21

**Later versions** of WM11 and 12 in F are found in British Library Add. 30310, in the composer's autograph full score dated to *c*. 1722 (see pp. 36, 39).

## Printed sources

*6 Ouvertures for Violins in all their Parts as they were perform'd at the King's Theatre in the Operas Theseus, Amadis, Pastor Fido, Admeto, Water Musick, Julius Caeser/ the 3.^d Collection. London, Walsh and . . . Hare* (contains the Overture only), *c*. 1725.

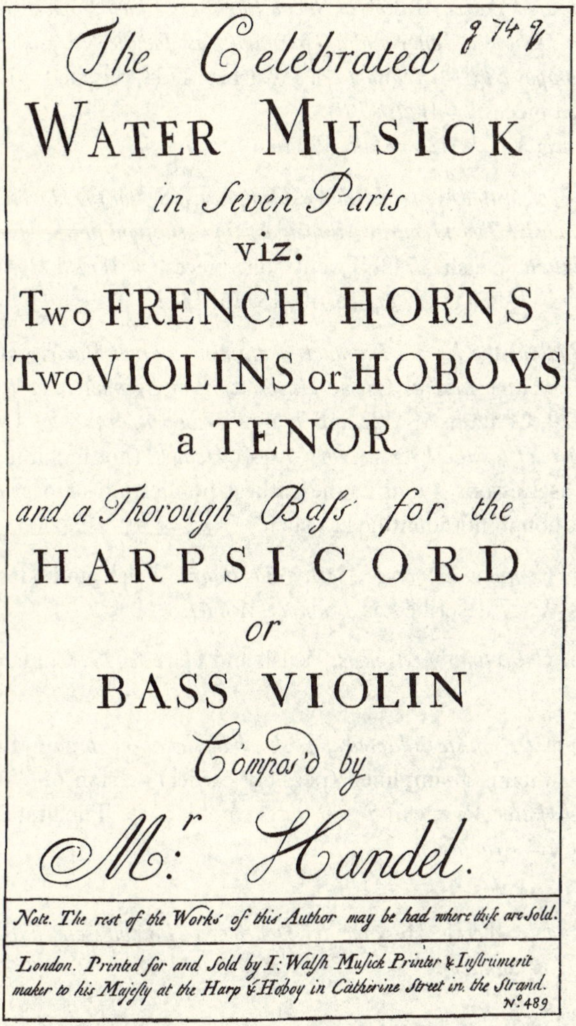

The Celebrated ʒ 74 ʒ

# WATER MUSICK
*in Seven Parts*

viz.

Two FRENCH HORNS

Two VIOLINS or HOBOYS

a TENOR

*and a Thorough Bass for the*

# HARPSICORD

*or*

# BASS VIOLIN

*Compas'd by*

## Mᴿ Handel.

*Note. The rest of the Works of this Author may be had where these are Sold.*

*London. Printed for and Sold by I: Walsh Musick Printer & Instrument maker to his Majesty at the Harp & Hoboy in Catherine Street in the Strand.*
*Nᵒ 489*

Plate 3  Title-page of *The Celebrated Water Musick in Seven Parts*, published by John Walsh *c.* 1733

*The Celebrated Water Musick in Seven Parts, viz. Two French Horns Two Violins or Hoboys a Tenor and a Thorough Bass for the Harpsicord or Bass Violin Compos'd by Mr Handel* ..., Walsh, *c*. 1733, reissued *c*. 1750. Ten numbered pieces ( = *Walsh PP*).

 *Sequence*: 3, 5, 9–12, 16, 17, 13, 14

*Handel's/ celebrated Water Musick / Compleat./ Set for the Harpsicord./ To which is added,/ Two favourite Minuets,/ with Variations for the Harpsicord,/ By Geminiani*. Walsh, 1743. Twenty-one pieces ( = *Walsh Hpd*).

 *Sequence*: 1–9, 11, 12, 22, 16, 17, 13–15, 18–21

*The 3d Book of the Lady's Banquet, containing a great Variety of the most pleasant and airy Lessons for the Harpsichord or Spinnet* ..., Walsh and Hare, 1720. Contains WM22 and 7, as *A Trumpet Minuet by Mr Hendell* and *A Minuet for the French Horn by Mr Hendell* (not including the 'B' section) as Lessons 1 and 2; the earliest publication of part of *Water Music*, although not identified as such.

*The New Country Dancing Master 3d Book*, Walsh and Hare, 1728. Contains WM7 described as *Trumpet Minuet*.

*A General Collection of Minuets*, Walsh and Hare, 1729. Contains WM7 and 22.

*Handel's water music adapted for the harpsichord or organ*, Longman, *c*. 1769. Contains a simplified (possibly earlier) version of WM11 *The celebrated Water Musick in Score* ..., Arnold, 1788. The first edition in full score ( = *Arnold*).

 *Sequence*: 1–22

*G. F. Händel's Werke: Ausgabe der Deutschen Händelgesellschaft*, vol. 47, 1886 ( = *Chrysander*).

 *Sequence*: 1–22

The earliest surviving sources (*RSM, Malmesbury, Drexel*) give a sequence that intersperses the trumpet numbers throughout the second half of the piece, and this order is preserved by *Arnold* and *Chrysander*; it is also possible that Arnold had access to manuscripts now lost to confirm this arrangement. Anthony Hicks has suggested that behind *Water Music* as we know it may lie a concerto in F (similar to Op. 3 no. 4) plus a dance suite in G (which he speculates may have formed the ballet for knights and ladies prescribed in the libretto of *Amadigi*, but not present in any score), into which Handel inserted new movements with brass.[6] This would certainly chime with the earliest sources, and suggests that the later sequences given in *Granville, Lennard* and Walsh's 1733 and 1743 publications (followed by *HHA* and *Fiske*), offering a division into three suites by key, were introduced for the convenience of those who needed only a selection of the material to form a normal-size suite. (Another modern theory tidily proposes that the three 'suites' can be attached to three different water parties; *HHA* gives 1715, 1717 and 1736.) The first is almost the date given by Mainwaring, though there is no mention of Handel's participation; the second is well documented; and the third, the eve of the wedding of the Prince of Wales and the Princess of Saxe-Gotha, 26 April 1736, when the couple 'passed the evening on the water with music', is not possible since some of the proposed suite was already in print before that date.

None of the three suggested re-groupings displays a convincing 'suite' design as it stands. Even allowing for what *New Grove* daringly calls Handel's 'technique bordering on laziness', the form is too lax: the F major suite has no end, the G major 'Flute Suite' no opening and it is difficult to attribute any purpose to WM10 other than to make a transition from F major to D major. *Malmesbury* attempts to solve the F major problem by repeating WM3 after WM9, but since that lengthy movement has already been heard twice, this smacks of expediency. *Aylesford* more judiciously moves WM7 to the end of the sequence. Even Walsh's problematic publication leaves the title in the singular and diplomatically announces: 'A Choice Sett of Aires, call'd Handel's Water Piece, composed in Parts for a Variety of Instruments'.

Handel seems to have taken little interest in the suite as a form, confining it to didactic keyboard works, extended overtures such as that for *Rodrigo*, or the dance sequences in *Terpsicore, Radamisto* and *Ariodante* designed to support theatre ballet. In opera Handel warmed to the programmatic and theatrical opportunities of an integrated ballet, which gave a chance for unusual sequences and tonalities. Here we find key schemes which move quite radically, unlike a normal suite. *Ariodante*, for instance, moves through E, A minor, C, A, E minor, and although the *Rodrigo* ballet music is all in B flat, it follows an unusual sequence of Gigue, Sarabande, Matelot (a gavotte), Menuet I, Bourée I and II, Menuet II, Passacaille.[7]

The named dance forms used in *Water Music* are of a few basic types: minuet, bourrée, the 'country dance' (a very English jig) and the hornpipe, more a rhythmic pattern than a dance form (hence 'alla hornpipe'). The Menuet, Minuet or Menuetto (Handel was careful with his terminology) was danced to a unit two bars long (i.e. in 6/4), so every second bar is unaccented (a point frequently neglected in performance). The simplest minuets were usually composed in $8 + 8$ bars, or multiples, but WM18 has a second section of 12 bars which better suits the pattern of minuet dance steps. Collections such as *Handel's Favourite Minuets* were published, some of the contents adapted from opera arias, others apparently newly composed; and more than a hundred minuets are listed in the HWV catalogue, mostly under keyboard music, which constitute a forgotten aspect of Handel's everyday composing life. They reveal a large repertoire of light music created, as the title-pages of the published collections state, for 'the Balls at Court, the Masquerades and Public Entertainment'.[8]

The Bourée (Boree, or in Germany often Bourrée), described as 'gay' by Rousseau and 'content and self-composed' by Mattheson (*Der vollkommene Capellmeister*, 1739), was so similar to the rigaudon that Quantz felt they were identical; but Handel's rigaudons are more angular and vigorously syncopated. When Bach uses pairs of bourrées in his three orchestral suites, they are indicated as 'da capo' (A–B–A), but in the absence of specific instructions this does not necessarily follow for Handel.

Handel recycled some of his earliest allemandes as rigaudons: the first Allemande in the dance music from *Daphne* (HWV 353) turns up as a rigaudon in *Radamisto*. To Mattheson it also suggested marine or pastoral scenes for the theatre, so for Handel it may have held some special appropriateness for a water party. The abrupt and short phrases of WM17 seem mirrored by Gottlieb Muffat's Rigaudon in his *Componimenti* (1726) and Handel's movement ends similarly, with an abrupt syncopation on the second beat of the bar.

The Hornpipe (a 'longways country dance') was associated with the British Isles, but not the sea. It had featured, often as the last movement of a suite, in the theatre and keyboard music of Locke, Purcell and their English contemporaries, and by Handel's time had gathered a quirky and care-free connotation, sometimes under the title of a Maggott, Whim or Delight.

Later in the eighteenth century the dancing master John Gallini said that people still flocked to London to 'apply themselves with great attention to the study of the Hornpipe' which was thought to be 'original to this country' (1770), despite the fact that the late eighteenth-century dance was very different from the syncopated Purcellian-Handelian model.

The Gigue Loure ( = WM16), a slow gigue or 'Spanish Gigue', has a typical two-note upbeat which, if bowed according to the rules of Georg Muffat, would leave an articulation, a sort of hiccup, at the barline (see Ex. 3.14, p. 42). François Couperin directs the Loure in *Les gouts-réunis* to be played 'pesamment', and Bach's C sharp minor prelude in Book I of the *Well-tempered Clavier* is a loure in all but name. J. C. Smith myster-iously calls the *Water Music* example a 'March'.

All music for dancing requires many repeats and the instructions in some *Water Music* sources to play a movement 'trois fois' sometimes include suggestions for varied scoring. Triple repeats were already familiar to English keyboard players from the keyboard suites of Draghi and were advocated for fast dances by Georg Muffat (*Ausserlesene Instrumental-Music*, Passau 1701). They may even be needed in Corelli's Op. 1 no. 4. In some of these instances the first-, second- and third-time endings show that each individual segment was played three times. With Handel we assume he means 'the whole dance three times', but there is scope for experiment here, as there is with da capos of dance pairs. Following the instructions for multiple repeats and adopting the recommended eighteenth-century tempi for these dances, the total playing length of the sequence comes very close to the 'one hour' reported by Bonet, showing that he is describing the whole piece, not separated extracts.

## *Water Music* in performance

Handel chose to open his entertainment with a style of **Overture** which would have sounded reassuringly familiar to his older listeners. The insistent rhythmic pattern of Ex. 3.1 is exploited in every bar of the opening section except the final cadence. The gesture may have been wasted on his royal master, since the style was no longer very fashion-able, but for his English audience it would have carried an enormous resonance of Purcell and his contemporaries: the overtures and preludes to *Abdelazar, Dioclesian, The Double Dealer, Bonduca* and many more

Ex. 3.1

Ex. 3.2

examples use this mono-rhythmic style. Handel was certainly both aware of and (following Cousser's advice) respectful towards his English predecessors, which meant he was never averse to borrowing from them; as late as 1748 in the overture to *Susanna* he incorporated material from John Blow's *St Cecilia Ode* for 1684.[9]

The subject of the ensuing fugue is found in a keyboard version of about this date, but in E major (HWV 612) and with a quite different continuation (see Ex. 3.2). It forms a well-calculated organic continuation of the opening section here, with the outline of a rising fourth common to both (see arrows), though in truth the movement is carried more by the later extensions of its new countersubject and by the episodes for oboes[10] and solo violins than by the full opening theme. At the pedal point (bar 57) Handel obviously feels doubtful that sufficient tension can be generated by using the first three notes of the subject alone and increases the temperature with all-purpose semiquaver figuration for the cellos and bassoons; the result is an energetic but messy texture.

For about eight years the overture alone circulated in Walsh's print (the only section of *Water Music* available in more or less full parts); first and second time endings were added, allowing a repeat of the fugue and a full cadence in F, whereas for the keyboard version a very clumsy cadence in the home key was tacked on (see Ex. 3.3a and b). The early issues of Walsh's parts included the following Adagio, WM2, which also ends in the dominant, thus merely postponing the problem; in the British Library copy of this set the Air (WM6) has been added in MS – a neat solution for a performance without horns.

Handel in fact ends in the dominant and segues to the entry of his first true soloist in the **Adagio e staccato (WM2)**. Several of his earlier operas

Ex. 3.3

had contained scenes where the expressive oboe precedes, and sometimes almost upstages, the singer in a slow aria. Here Handel dispenses with any soprano and leaves the oboe with a free (though surely not unmeasured) hand at decorating a skeletal line. Exactly the same scheme, scoring, rhythms and contours can be found reused nearly thirty years later when Handel produced what amounts to a 'parody' of this movement in the overture to the *Occasional Oratorio* (1746); it must have been one of the many 'templates' he kept by him all his life. There are three problems in the *Water Music* movement as we have it: the first is the consecutive fifths between violin and viola in bar 6, easily corrected by changing the viola D to a C and thus preserving the repeated harmonies of the previous bars. Then there is the potentially unbalanced cadence at bars 16–17 where the solo oboe appears to be accompanied by all the bass instruments, solved by slimming the bass line in performance. Least tractable is the meaningless state of the viola line immediately following in all sources.

Least tractable is the meaningless state of the viola line immediately following in almost all the sources. The most reliable scores (*RSM*, *Granville*, *Lennard*) give three bars rest and crotchets in bar 20 which do not fit, and the revised entry proposed by *Arnold*, *Chrysander* and most modern editions in bar 21 is patently impossible. The reading of the *Aylesford* score shows that there should be only two bars rest, with bar 20 repeating bar 19 a tone lower (Ex. 3.4). A further change, proposed in *Fiske*, is to move the two violin I notes in bar 18 to the Viola part; although this reading is found in no surviving source, it certainly creates a convincing viola line and a logical entry for Violin I in bar 19.

Ex. 3.4

Handel's best theatrical stroke is withholding the novel entry of two horns until the following **Allegro (WM3)**. With reiterated signals and bravura lip-trills, which surely continue on all long notes, there is an air of outdoor confidence to this show-piece, with the jaunty rhythms of the hornpipe added unexpectedly in bars 80ff., developing into a full skirmish of conventional battle/storm figuration in bar 91 and again at the close. All editions worry over the conflicting rights of the two rhythmic patterns ♫ ♩ and ♫ ♩ which are confused and inconsistent in every source.

The contrasting **Andante (WM4)** might have been a movement for solo organ and strings in a later period. The wind band proposes a theme later heard in the sonata Op. 1 no. 6 (1724), where it is marked Andante larghetto, and then plays a sort of continuo accompaniment to the strings repeat. Equality of balance is of the essence here (multiple oboes are needed) in order to support the high register of some of the string writing (bars 10, 13, 23). A repeat of movement 3 is only specified in some sources, but convincingly unless preparation time is requested by the horns before movement 5.

Several movements in the *Water Music* selection show signs of having a separate existence as horn duos, and indeed were eventually published in that form in 1733: *Forrest Harmony, Book the Second being ... several Curious Pieces out of the* Water Musick, *made on purpose for two French Horns, By the Greatest Masters* contains WM17 with a nicely decorated penultimate bar, WM5 complete with echoes and the whole of WM11 with the two parts swapped on each repeat to represent the alternation of trumpets and horns. **WM5** is probably an orchestrated expansion of such a duo, as heard in the final six bars of each section. The second horn suffers in the process, with a clashing harmony in bar 3, and a loss of leading role in 26ff., thanks to the part now being doubled by the bass line. The movement is sometimes described as a Passepied, a type of fast minuet, although it lacks the usual upbeat for this dance, but a gentle tempo (maybe the 'Allegro' of *RSM*) seems more probable than the 'Presto' proposed solely in *Aylesford*.

On the other hand the 'Presto' suggested in *Aylesford* and later printed sources for the following **Air (WM6)** will be more than welcomed by generations of listeners bored by the sentimental and even funereal tradition. The written dotted rhythms are surely a notated form of French *notes inégales*, proven by Handel himself forgetting to write them in bar 25 of the full version, and more tellingly, in the final bars of his keyboard transcription (Ex. 3.5). This is the only item from *Water Music* which we have in his own hand, a keyboard arrangement preserved in the Fitzwilliam Museum, Cambridge (Music MUS 260, p. 11) and dating from *c*. 1725.

The differences are instructive for the performer and also indicative of the fluid state in which Handel's music must have existed in his memory, as a sonic trace, full of possibilities for re-use and transformation, rather than a visual imprint in final form. This keyboard adaptation comes after arrangements of part of the overture to *Il Pastor Fido* (1712*)* and the overture to *Amadigi* (1715) in the same MS, all possibly projected for inclusion in keyboard suites. The rhythmic changes are telling and suggest underdotting or *notes inégales* in performance. The inspired addition of a sustained horn note for the *double* (essentially one horn part divided between two players for breathing purposes) involves a tactful rewriting of bars 27–30 which had previously modulated into G minor, where the natural horn could not follow. Oboes are specified in *RSM* ('Vi: ob 1' and 'Viol ob 2') at the beginning of the movement, but given in *Lennard* ('Tutti Hautb: e violini') and *Shaftesbury* ('Tutti Oboe') only for this section, suggesting that they were not playing earlier.

*Arnold* (and, following him, *Chrysander*) begins **WM7** with a sixteen-bar introduction for the two horns alone, as given in *Malmesbury* and *Drexel* but rejected by *Fiske*, which could certainly have been the original

*Altered by Handel from D.

Ex. 3.5

duo version of the piece. *RMS* not only includes these horn parts, but also interpolates two eight-bar sections for two oboes and bassoon after bars 8 and 16 which are not found in any other source. Possibly this minuet existed in several scorings and Handel's original material may have shown two such versions side by side which the copyist decided to amalgamate (a similar transformation of a minuet can be seen comparing the oboe sonata

Ex. 3.6

Op. 1 no. 5 with the concerto Op. 3 no. 4). In its wind version, however, the present minuet is coherent and deserves consideration if not incorporation (see Ex. 3.6).

The addition of orchestral parts to the horn duo, as in WM5, creates some difficulties of harmony, including an outright dissonance from the repeated Gs of Horn II in bar 29 which is included without comment in every version. If Handel had actually intended the horns to play with the orchestra, he must have accepted a harmonic solecism here which occurs rarely in his music. Perhaps the horns originally played *in alternation* with the tutti, which is self-sufficient, and were conflated by a copyist.

Respite for the brass is offered with a trio in the 'forlorn' key of F minor and the device of a middle-register melody (violin II, viola, bassoon) plus a first violin descant, familiar from Bach's Suite 1 and Telemann's orchestral writing, and found again in the Country Dance in *Water Music* as well as the movement from Handel's Op. 3 no. 4 which found its way into the 'Oxford' version of *Water Music* (see below, p. 47). Since the violins are unable to follow the melody down to a low F in bar 47, we must assume either an earlier version of the piece at least a tone higher, or an alternative orchestration. *Arnold* and all editions since except *Fiske* conceal the point by rewriting this bar. Several keyboard adaptations of this section ignore the actual melody and foolishly present only the descant violin part (*Walsh*

*Hpd*, etc.) and in *Malmesbury* it is marked 'Adagio'; a MS version HWV 547 (transposed to A) offers a better solution by omitting the descant. The da capo indicated in most sources would presumably be played without repeating the horn introduction.

The following two movements are both to be heard '3 times: – First all the Violins, – $2^d$. all the Hautboys, – $3^d$. all together', as *RSM*, *Granville* and *Lennard* put it. The absence of the viola line in the second scoring is little loss in the **Bourrée (WM8)** and only a slight sorrow in the **Hornpipe (WM9)**, where it crosses the second violin/oboe line insensitively. The melodic construction of the Bourrée is a fine example of *perfidia*, the use of a single device to deliberate excess so appreciated by the Italians. Hardly a single bar is without a falling second: the first three and the last five are almost nothing but. The same feature is taken over, less obsessively, in the Hornpipe, but although they are thus linked thematically, the effect of two successive movements in identical scoring (which Handel has avoided thus far in *Water Music*) is not cumulative enough to be an effective end to a putative 'Suite in F'. It also lacks the distinctive presence of the horns, a major drawback in a 'Horn Suite'. A possible modern solution, not offered in any original source, is to end with Handel's later versions of WM11 and 12 in F major, both featuring the horns. Handel's *Water Music* solution is to proceed with a linking movement of totally different character to prepare the way for D major as the horns change their crooks and the trumpets are ushered in for the first time.

**WM10** has no tempo indication, but is so reminiscent of 'The flocks shall leave the mountains' in *Acis and Galatea* of the following year that we can assume an Allegro moderato, pastoral but not sedentary. There are also echoes of a threatening Polyphemus ('Oh ruddier than the cherry') in the sequence of downward scales in bars 50–54, which adds motivation to the mobility. Since open-air performance makes antiphony well-nigh impossible, this movement, like its D minor companion WM4, relies on the alternation of the *due cori* – wind-band and string-band – to extend the scale and level of intent. The writing is more sophisticated than most of the other movements in *Water Music*, and could be dropped without incongruity into one of the Op. 3 concertos. One feels that Handel, for once, is attending to the needs of the connoisseurs in the water party. The independent bassoon part, the dovetailing of the two orchestras with stretto and the cadence deliberately given to one band alone to feature the entry of new material with a new sonority (bar 12), display a subtlety of construction not expected in *al fresco* music.

Even the final cadence in the tonic rather than the expected half-cadence (as heard already in movements 1, 2 and 4 and about to be used again to link 11 to 12) is well calculated to heighten the surprise of the sudden D major trumpet entry. Though full of virtues, it is beyond the powers of this movement to either end an F major suite or begin one in D major – thus it is superfluous in the 'three suite' scheme of things. The fact that this movement is missing from *Walsh Hpd* and other keyboard reductions is simply because the overlapping alternations between winds and strings would be meaningless on a single keyboard, but its presence in *Malmesbury* suggests that it was part of the original sequence.

From this point in the suite both the scoring and the changes of tonality become more varied, a strategy that seems designed to maintain attention through an hour-long performance – the length of a full act in opera, but no other musical form to date.

The regal key of D major, with its increased possibilities of antiphony between trumpets and horns, begins with a prelude (**WM11**) that suggests a hasty improvisation, or at least a portmanteau method of construction (rather like the German language) where each unit is different, but modifies or complements its neighbour. The military opening is borrowed from a rescue aria in Keiser's *La forza della virtù* (see Ex. 3.7).

The various units are presented in the simplest form of trumpet statement answered *notatim* an octave lower by the horns. Natural trumpets did not play in F, but horns crooked in D could offer an answer to the trumpets an octave lower. There is no hint of development; a new phrase is offered, and repeated ditto, the variety simply being in the length of phrase chosen. Handel groups his units unpredictably: 8 bars, a half bar, 2 bars, 4 bars, 1 bar, 2 bars, 4 bars, all given in high scoring and then repeated in the lower orchestration. A very nominal move towards the dominant (bars 26–8) is soon contradicted and we fall back to the tonic, feeling that there is something a little too formulaic about the process, until Handel opts to forgo antiphony and return with a variant on the opening figure, scored for full brass, as a 'grand chorus' to end. He then neatly varies this with repeated quavers in place of the dotted crotchet and a linking scale in bar 41 to paper over the join and create

Ex. 3.7

the impression of a wider and grander landscape than mere repetition would allow. Putting aside the effect of brilliant brass scoring, the sensation is of banality narrowly avoided by the final eight tutti bars. The final bars, modulating in a phrygian cadence, warn that a da capo is probable. Luckily, Handel moves on to the Hornpipe.

A later version of this and the following number in Handel's own autograph (British Library Add. 30310) dates from about 1722, and these movements presumably formed all or part of the 'New Concerto with French Horns' announced for performance at Drury Lane on 20 March 1723. The revisions give some indication of the power of Handel's self-criticism. Literal repetition is avoided in this new F major version, since only the horns are available, and an altogether more thoughtful version of very similar material is offered. We find variation of the opening motive as soon as bar 5 where Ex. 3.8 turns into Ex. 3.9 for the solo horns (the idiomatic *portato* articulation marked by Handel). There is a clearer delineation of tutti versus solo for the half-bar phrases in bars 9 and 10, and a new and unexpected texture created for a long tutti from 15 with active violins, horns

Ex. 3.8

Ex. 3.9

reiterating their solo patterns of quavers and oboes and (independent) bassoons sustaining separate lines of pungent suspensions, where in the D major version they had simply doubled the violins. Now a middle section is created, given to strings alone, dominated by violin *bariolage* and offering relief for and from the winds; new tonalities beyond the scope of the horns can be explored, and the non-stop semiquavers of the violins (albeit generic patterns) add a broader sense of scale to the piece, justifying a full da capo. Far from being a version simply differing in 'thematic details' as described in *Redlich*, it absolves Handel from the easier but superficially showier solutions he adopted in D major.

The **Hornpipe (WM12)** is possibly the most memorable movement of the whole collection, combining instrumental brilliance and rhythmic vitality in a way which carries more forward momentum than the preceding introduction. As with WM11, we may suspect an earlier origin for this catchy theme, although it has not yet been identified. Certainly all the elements (except the persistent syncopations of the second part) had already been heard in *Amadigi* two years previously in the hero's Act III aria, 'Sento la gioia, ch'in sen mi brilla' (see Ex. 3.10).

From this outburst of confidence and swagger, and its contrafactum in *Water Music*, one could extrapolate the possible basic form of such a hornpipe, simply by removing the repetitions that Handel employs (see Ex. 3.11). Whether or not some such *Ur*-Hornpipe ever existed (possibly in an English source), the reduction clarifies the modular means of extension

Ex. 3.10

and repetition Handel used according to the resources to hand. With expanded contrasts of horns and trumpets as well as tutti orchestra he could revisit the same material three times, and he does so without shame. These units are as varied in length as those of WM11; the

Ex. 3.11

difference is that they all belong to a coherent whole and follow a natural sequence of modulation. The result is, frankly, better composition.

The later F major version with only horns and winds is not the 'exact transposition' of the D major movement, as described in *Redlich*, p. vii. There is no call for improved coherence, and Handel opts to have the oboe band take over the trumpet exchanges almost literally, simply adding a bassoon bass. But he integrates an extra two-bar exchange in the A section (bars 34–8), and with singular imagination seizes the chance on the join to suggest a long note counter-melody to the repeated note motive which is found nowhere in the D major version but

Ex. 3.12

pre-echoes the *cantus firmus* effect of 'For the Lord God' in the Hallelujah Chorus, fulfilling exactly the same role of consolidating a lot of excited but fragmentary repetition around it (see Ex. 3.12).

In both the D and F major versions, the middle section of the Hornpipe has exactly the same bar-count (and shares figuration with the second movement of Handel's later recorder/flute sonata Op. 1 no. 9). The F major version contains innumerable variants in local detail and lacks the third violin part which seems to have been included in the D major version in case the oboes were missing. There is again no need for re-writing since the D major performs its job ideally of restoring a sense of longer vision after the exchange of short fragments in part one; there are only two internal cadences, and the running violin quavers carry the argument unbroken for eighteen bars (to the dominant), ten bars back to the tonic, and a spacious coda of nine bars. Woven amongst the running quavers are

lost in the nineteenth century: 'it contains various airs, choruses, capricios, fugues, and other pieces of music, with the names of contemporary musicians, such as Zackau, Alberti, Frobergher, Krieger, Kerl, Ebner, Strunch. They were probably exercises adopted at pleasure, or dictated for him to work upon, by his master. The composition is uncommonly scientific, and contains the seeds of many of his subsequent performances.'[20] By 'performances' Coxe presumably had improvisations in mind, although we may now surmise that these 'seeds' also germinated in notated compositions.

Some exchange was mutual, as Telemann reports from Handel's early days: 'In fashioning subjects of melody, Handel and I were continually exercising our fancy, and reciprocally communicating our thoughts, both by letter and conversation, in the frequent visits we made to each other.'[21] Although we assume this refers to their earliest period of acquaintance, before Handel left Germany, there must have been continuing communication throughout Handel's life. One of the last letters he wrote was to Telemann about a lost consignment of rare plants (tomatoes?).

While a lot is currently made of Handel's reliance on material from Telemann, there is curiously little comment when Bach acts similarly, lifting the whole opening ritornello of the slow movement of his A major harpsichord concerto (BWV 1055) – both melody and the distinctive *pizzicato* accompaniment – directly from a concerto by the same composer.[22] Yet the importance of the 'borrowed' material here could be construed as more crucial and fundamental than Handel's borrowings, since for Bach the construction of the opening ritornello was the essence of the composition. Almost everything else could be extrapolated from this 'tectonic nucleus',[23] whereas Handel would adapt his opening ritornello throughout the process of composition, adding and subtracting, moving phrases and units around (even making half-bar shifts) and compressing by excision without replacement. 'Surgery', as Paul Brainard puts it, 'was for him part and parcel of the composition process itself.'[24]

This casual treatment of smaller units, as well as reducing his 'culpability' for those who care, enhances our view into Handel's musical processes at the most detailed level. Handel's units are more '*moduli*' than '*Figuren*' – we might almost call them 'clichés' and grant them the immunity of anonymity. A writer might describe them as the everyday language of gesture or the 'recognisable phrase': Roland Barthes rounds off the circle by equating the 'figure' with a 'sign' or even, in music, 'a vocal incipit'.[25] A fascination with the small detail and 'cut-and-paste' methods was certainly not unique to Handel. Paul Klee's definition of his technique ('Andacht zum Kleinen' – devotion to small things) is instructive, though Handel adds to that a congenital addiction to canvases more on the scale of Rubens. Closer to Handel's own time, Mattheson describes the process in detail as a normal compositional technique:

> For the theme or principal melody [of a composition], which in the science of melody represents what the text or subject is to an orator, certain formulas must be held in reserve, that can be employed in general [musical] discourse. That is to say: the composer, through much experience and attentive listening to good works, must have collected here and there modulations, little turns, clever motives [*Fälle*], pleasing figures, conjunct and leaping, which, though consisting only of merely detached things, can bring about something general and complete through suitable combination. If, for example, I should have the three following different and separate passages in mind:

> and out of them I wished to make one cohesive phrase, it could appear something like the following:

> For though one or other of these motives and turns might have already been used by other masters and might occur to me without thinking of the first composer or knowing who it was, still this combination can be considered as a unique invention. Also, it is not necessary to do such intentionally; it can occur by chance.
> These details should not be taken so as to suggest that one should write down a kind of index of such fragments and, according to school rules, make a regular invention box out of them; but proceed in the same way as we build up a reserve of words and expressions for speaking, not necessarily on paper or in a book, but in our heads and thoughts. By this means

our ideas, be they spoken or written down, can easily be brought to light without always consulting a dictionary.

True, whoever wants and needs to, can always prepare such a written down collection of fine passages and modulations which he runs into here and there, and which please him, organised under certain main sections and titles, so that in requisite cases, he can take [from it] necessary counsel and comfort. However, a lame and botched arrangement will probably result, if one's clumsy melody is patched together from such bits, even if they were of silver and gold.

Now because such available and special 'moduli' offer good assistance in the formation of a main theme, which we are talking about here, on the other hand we are led from certain general things in the art of invention to the particular: namely where one can use ordinary and familiar things for special purposes. For example, cadences are something common and are met in every musical piece. But they can occur right at the beginning of a particular main theme, though otherwise they belong at the close.[26]

Handel could use Mattheson's process to dashing effect. He transformed the overture to the *Ode for St Cecilia's Day* into a concerto opening simply by tacking on, as a *modulus*, some tirades for solo violin (Op. 6 no. 5) – and this well before Mozart's more publicised K.271 where the soloist also speaks early. The insertions of 'Wonderful, Counsellor' in *Messiah*, the unaltered Telemann quotations in the incidental figuration of the overture to the *Occasional Oratorio* – these and many more are examples of what Winton Dean splendidly termed 'grouting'. This is more dramatic than a simple *ars combinatoria*, since Handel developed a larger-scale modular construction than Mattheson conceived. *The Arrival of the Queen of Sheba*, for example, draws together Telemann (six bars from the Allegro of the Concerto in *Musique de table* II), three bars from his own Overture for two clarinets and horn, another fifteen bars from the aria in Porta's *Numitore* on which he based his clarinet overture, and a Muffat keyboard gigue. Handel gave no sign of wanting to conceal what he was doing. At the end of his life he not only openly arranged his own music, but based *La Réjouissance* on arias by Porta both heard and published in London.

Sometimes his transferences seem to deny the theory of *Affekt*. A fugal sketch shows that the theme that eventually became 'Let all the angels of God' had been tried for the quite contrary sentiment of 'And cast away their yokes from us'. In the same oratorio those choruses made from Handel's earlier Italian duet cantatas owe all their scansion and coloratura to the original amorous text ('No, di voi non vuo' fidarmi') rather than that of *Messiah*, hence the upsetting accentuation of 'FOR unto us a Child is born'.

Knowledge of these antecedents should affect our reactions to Handel's *music* as little as remembering the most banal early version of a Beethoven theme in sketchbook form when listening to a finished symphony, yet for anyone with an interest in Handel's *mind* it provides an almost limitless avenue of speculation. As Chrysander remarked, 'I readily acknowledge that these borrowings of his, which inspire anxiety in certain people, are a source of instruction and pleasure to me, which I would not want to be without at any price.'[27]

Handel saw the grand plan and used whatever bricks came his way to build it. Keeping company with writers, painters and architects rather than musicians may have helped form his conscience here: Walter Emery pointed out that 'such procedure was nothing unusual in an age when Flitcroft could borrow Gibbs's [1721] design for the steeple of St. Martin-in-the-Fields, and re-use it [ten years later], with minor "improvements", no further away than St. Giles's'.[28] Like Hogarth, Handel's ideal of beauty was a calculated 'uniformity amidst variety' rather than the reverse (which was Bach's technique), though we have yet to discover whether for Handel there was an equivalent of Hogarth's secret 'serpentine line' of construction.[29] In literature the sincerest form of flattery has always been admitted; the multiplicity of sources for the libretto of *Acis and Galatea* was never investigated nor even challenged. As T. S. Eliot put it, 'Immature artists imitate; mature artists steal', and he lived up to the precept himself, borrowing whole sequences of 'The Coming of the Magi' *verbatim* from the 1622 Christmas Day sermon of Bishop Lancelot Andrewes. With Handel it is a matter of adopting points rather than whole procedures, or, to fit Walpole's happy horti-cultural metaphor, plants rather than plans: 'Ought one man's garden to be deprived of a happy object, because that object has been employed by another?'[30]

The writer today is expected to give notice of his 'influences', the painter expects them to be discerned with approbation by cognoscenti, but the composer has no method of admission for anything more subtle than 'Variations on a Theme by X'. Those who today find Handel's

methods slightly immoral are often reacting to the wholescale enthusiasm with which he employed them – a lifetime commitment to crime
rather than a momentary lapse: 'he was borrowing from Bononcini in
1702, certainly from Keiser in 1707, then from all and sundry up to 1751,
when in *Jephtha* he is reworking arias by Galuppi written only the year
before'.[31] But if the technique is admissible *and* effective, it would be a
timid writer who did not exploit it fully. While Handel was unusual in
the amount of material he borrowed, there is no sign that he ever tried to
conceal or deny it; the 'obscurity' of some of his choices reflects more our
ignorance than his guile.

In a sense, *all* Handel is a form of borrowing and arrangement. When
are we ever sure we are hearing the real *first* version? To return to our
opening metaphor, Handel had all the virtues of Jonathan Swift's bee
which 'by an universal Range, with long Search, much Study, true
Judgment, and Distinction of Things, brings home Honey and Wax'.[32]

# 5

## *The* Concerti a due cori

Tho' no man ever introduced such a number of instruments, yet in his Orchestra not one is found idle or insignificant.

(Mainwaring, *Memoirs*, p. 202)

The three 'Double Concertos' or *Concerti a due cori* are the least discussed and most rarely performed of Handel's mature orchestral pieces. Yet they are perfect demonstrations of the composer's large-scale originality and small-scale ingenuity, and mostly created with pre-existing material.

As ever with Handel, they reflect a composer of circumstance, and were sparked by commercial pressure and the public mood. Audiences were central to Handel's aesthetic calculations, and for reasons beyond his control his oratorio season was no longer drawing. War had been dragging on for nearly ten years, initially in 1739 with Spain, later involving France and Prussia. Britain was drawn in from 1742, when the King led his own troops into battle at Dettingen (the last time a British monarch undertook such a role, though wicked rumour said his horse had simply bolted) and secured a grand victory, celebrated at home with Handel's *Dettingen Te Deum*. Handel then declared his independence from the political machine and reiterated that he was determined to 'write for himself'. The immediate outcome was *Semele*, composed in 1743, a new and precariously secular story. It was a dangerous standpoint to adopt, and Christopher Smith wondered 'how the Quality will take it that He can compose for Himself and not for them when they offered him more than ever he had in his Life'.[1] In 1745 came a second and closer military threat with the Jacobite rebellion. Handel, after suffering a disastrous concert season because of the latest military distractions, was quick to react with the hastily assembled *Occasional Oratorio* and a cheering *Song for the Gentlemen Volunteers of the City of London*. When the rebels were routed, two 'military oratorios' followed: *Judas Maccabeus* – dedicated to the victorious commander, 'Butcher Cumberland', the son of George II – and *Joshua*. In these military 'allegories', Britain was identified by many people as the 'new Jerusalem', a 'second and better Israel'.[2] Themes of Jewish patriotism and victory gave a hint of security and abundance replacing years of violence and uncertainty, all thanks to Hanoverian solidarity.

In this context, and perhaps mindful of Smith's warning, Handel conducted what appears to us as one of his most daring experiments, but in the form of novelty interval music:

> At the Theatre-Royal … this day … will be perform'd a New Oratorio, call'd JUDAS MACCHABEUS. *With a New* CONCERTO …
>
> (*General Advertiser*, 1 April 1747)

HWV 334 has been identified as being this new work, the earliest of the *Concerti a due cori*.

There is no evidence of a specific outside model for these works.[3] Vivaldi's *concerti per molti strumenti* are the nearest in colouring, but they lack Handel's large-scale architectural plan, and his six experiments in antiphony called *Concerti a due cori* (RV 581–5 and RV 793) are for two antiphonal orchestras either side of a church nave. Perhaps there is no need to look for a model. Handel's speciality was the 'grand plan', to which he fitted the individual elements: he had devised a river suite in several keys lasting an hour and had essentially invented the English oratorio and the organ concerto. If Bach can have 'Concerts à Plusieurs Instruments' (as the *Brandenburg Concertos* were described), why not from Handel a 'concerto for several orchestras'?

The antiphonal conceit employed in these concertos is only possible in an enclosed space where the placement can be accurately and stereophonically heard, as Gabrieli and the earlier Venetians knew. This is by definition *not* outdoor music – the *Concerti a due cori* employ fewer brass than *Water Music* or *Fireworks Music* and much of the argument is carried by the strings alone. For the best antiphonal effect in the theatre, we can imagine the strings being placed centrally on the stage with the two *cori* – wind bands, plus two pairs of horns in HWV 333 and 334 – at either side, or even in the boxes.

'Block dialogue' was not a normal constituent of high Baroque writing. Double choruses are rare in Handel ('Lift up your heads', *Israel in Egypt*, *Solomon*) and in the *Concerti a due cori* Handel innovates still further by extending the concept to instrumental groupings, labelled 'Chorus 1' and 'Chorus 2', *plus* a supporting orchestra, creating a three-point balance of power. He had achieved grandeur in choral settings, and a transfer to instrumental formats might have seemed a natural step. It is doubtful if he would have been aware of the Venetian antecedents with *cori spezzati*, but such alternation is the perfect demonstration in music of affirmation and confidence. It is unfair to complain that such a construction can 'scarcely sound like a true concerto movement',[4] when Handel clearly wanted a change from the formats of suite, concerto grosso and organ concerto. Most importantly, one of his best inventions, the oratorio chorus, could now be turned to good use instrumentally. Handel again demonstrates his ability to see the potential for unexpected *structural* changes in pre-existing material, finding antiphony in four-part fugues, just as in *Messiah* he transformed vocal duets into full choruses to create 'For unto us', 'And he shall purify', etc. The autographs show that for the *due cori* he normally began by copying in the original choral music *notatim* and then adapting and rearranging it as he worked.

The various combinations and contrasts of Handel's groupings seem endless. At the most basic, he uses the full group homophonically, winds doubling strings and no antiphony. Then there are varieties of two-way exchange between the two *cori*, or between the pairs of horns, horns versus the remaining tutti, strings versus unison *cori* – all these and many other permutations occur, plus the insertion of solo oboe passages, and a new-found independence for the bassoons.

In addition to the strategies suggested by the scoring, Handel made other intriguing compositional decisions. As far as possible he avoided material which carried suggestions of a ritornello structure, which by its nature emphasises the paragraph-by-paragraph construction, and he cancelled the only *da capo* instruction in the set, thus avoiding wholescale repetition. Instead he looked to forward-moving, almost classical structures – fugues, grounds, and his own brand of improvisatory flow-of-consciousness – aiming at a word-free version of the continuous development he had already achieved in choruses, and concluding eventually that a chorus without its singers was the simplest solution.

The scale of the operation clearly attracted Handel. He intended – and needed – a combination of movements longer than his previous concertos (although we cannot be sure how extended his 'organo ad libitum' solos were in the later works). The scale even of one of the Op. 6 concerti grossi might have seemed quite puny if put alongside the sheer stature of later oratorios like *Solomon* and *Judas Maccabeus*.

The first published version of these *concerti* was attempted by Arnold in 1797, and later Chrysander. The results were muddled by missing sources for the 'third' concerto, and the supplement issued later when Chrysander was aware of the Fitzwilliam MS only partly corrects things. His numbering inadvertently established a false chronology; re-established in their correct order, these concertos show Handel moving *towards* rather than away from direct transcriptions. It is interesting that few borrowings have been traced in the first *Concerto in Judas Maccabeus*. He seems to have started experimenting with freshly generated material. Only later, when it was clear that the concept worked, did he decide that pre-existing choruses were ideal quarries for further concertos.[5]

## Concerto in Judas Maccabeus HWV 334 (1747)

The first work in this original form is the one based most clearly on antiphony and repetition, the obvious formulaic response to the scoring and thus the closest in strategy to the large-scale movements in *Water Music*. It also exists in an arrangement as an organ concerto, HWV 305a (and reduced to an organ solo, 305b), with the March from *Judas Maccabeus* as its fourth movement. As a keyboard concerto it was presumably also intended for insertion into oratorio intervals, with the organ taking the place of *both* the wind *cori* (to preserve one of the *cori*, as Chrysander proposed, results in impossible collisions between them and the soloist in the passages rewritten by Handel).

Handel begins the **Ouverture** with a self-quotation from a piece that has military overtones, the Overture in D for two clarinets and horn (HWV 424) dated some six years earlier, which is thought to have been written for the horn-player 'Mr. Charles the Hungarian' and two colleagues, who may well have had military backgrounds (see Ex. 5.1).

In the expanded scoring Handel can now develop the device of the triumphant rising scale, which is to be a feature of most of the victory

Ex. 5.1

Ex. 5.2

music, but was originally hidden by the clarinets falling back an octave in bar 3. Now the opening bars rise an octave and a half uninterrupted and even the bass-line supporting the oboe solos in Mvt 5 (bars 59ff.) follows this device. These twenty bars are totally homophonic, the first and last such movement in the concerto.

Rising arpeggios and scales are added for the **Allegro Mvt 2**; Handel's alterations and experiments with solo horn writing can be seen in the MS and he decides to cover some sections with added oboes. The energetic off-beat figure first heard at bar 13 will be reused at the opposite end of HWV 333/5, where it is introduced purely for the coda (bars 113ff.; see Ex. 5.2).

The head theme of the **Allegro ma non troppo (Mvt 3)** is derived from the textual rhythms of 'Lift up your heads', giving the impression of a vocal transcript though, as far as we know, it has no earlier form. Principally based on repetition and antiphony like WM11, with small but varied units throughout, it is given over to the two wind bands; the strings are present only from bar 63 to the end, where they give a much-needed, fuller-breathed continuity after rather too much predictable repetition of '*moduli*'. In fact, with such small scraps of affirmative exclamation, it can hardly be worth looking for an earlier source – the gesture is all that counts (although some added words might redeem the over-repetition). Handel deploys the same predictability as he had in WM11 – again, no repeat is varied – but this time writ larger and with a final amused nod at the single-bar phrases, showing how such scraps can be ingeniously incorporated to puncture the rhetoric of a large-scale tutti just where another composer might be resigned to a conventionally grandiose cadence.

The grave **Adagio (Mvt 4)**, appealing though it is, could have been lifted from any trio sonata; the viola part is in no sense vital, and the chief value of this movement here is purely architectural, a buffer between the competing fanfares of Mvt 3 and the prancing cavalry rhythms of **Mvt 5, Andante Larghetto**,[6] which are going to be heard again in *Fireworks Music*. The opening disposition is antiphonal wind bands, but when the strings enter in bar 19 the allocations change, with the winds of both bands and strings unified in opposition to the horns (occasionally in four parts, mostly doubling), tutti at bar 44 and solo oboe at 59. (Only the oboe of *Coro* 1 gets solos, which effectively redirect the efforts of the tutti.) This unexpected solo arrival is neatly dovetailed into short tuttis which then take over the triplets which were suggested by the oboe. A medley of new ideas, none followed far, is rounded off with a full ten bars of the opening *couplet*. The 'free rondo' form of this movement is the antithesis of Bach's structures where everything is contained in the opening ritornello. If reminiscent of anything, it would be a French chaconne with *couplets*; the episodes which sound so idiomatic to the oboe here derive from a quite separate source, the vocal roulades of 'The leafy honours' in *Belshazzar* which illustrate 'giddy dissipation'. The chaconne style would normally signal a finale, but it is capped with a 'gigue à la chasse', **Allegro Mvt 6**, suggesting that Handel was seeing the piece as more of a full suite than a concerto. Even so there is a risk of this finale sounding *de trop*, and Handel seems to have realised this – perhaps he was reminded by exhausted horn soloists – and cancelled a long middle section and da capo. One of his other alterations has lost us a pertinent marking: he indicated a crescendo on the long held notes with a sequence of 'p', 'pf' [poco forte] and 'f' over three beats, and doubtless expected the same later in the movement where this passage survives (bars 38–41). The extrovert mood and mannerisms, the combination of gigue rhythm and incorporated trills, call up memories of 'Happy We' from *Acis and Galatea* as well as the more direct borrowing from Rosmira's hunting aria 'Io seguo sol fiero tra boschi le belve' in *Partenope*.

## 'Concerto made from Choruses' HWV 332 (*Joshua*, 1748)

Smith identified this manuscript bluntly on the cover of the MS: 'Concerto made from Choruses' – in fact three choruses, plus the opening section of an overture (to be used twelve days later for *Alexander Balus*), and a concluding Minuet – to be given at the opening performance of *Joshua* on 9 May. No horns are used; they had already been heard in the oratorio (assuming the Concerto introduced Act III), but very specifically associated with the title role of the 'Conqu'ring Hero', and Handel presumably did not want to squander the effect.

The **Ouverture (Mvt 1)** speaks in an earlier English manner – it would hardly have been out of place introducing a Purcell ode – and is followed by 'And the Glory of the Lord' (**Allegro ma non troppo, Mvt 2**), another (to us) immediately recognisable highlight. (In the autograph, Handel originally placed this movement between nos. 6 and 7, then later added a 'Segue NB' to move it forwards.) As in *Messiah*, the splendid notion of introducing the opening fugue subject as a harmonised melody decoys the listener from any apprehensions of the complexities of a fugue structure based on three motives, open-webbed and declamatory as it is. Given its origin as a four-part chorus, there is no antiphony available for the *cori*: the oboes of both bands represent soprano and alto, bassoon I the tenor and bassoon II the vocal bass, a scheme which, depending on the numbers employed, can pose tricky questions of balance. Handel tries to add the violas to bassoon I whenever possible, but the novelty of hearing an independent bassoon line is sometimes offset by the problem of *not* hearing it. Alfred Mann has pointed out that where in the choral version Handel had created gradual combinations of his three subjects ('And the glory', 'shall be revealed' and 'for the mouth of the Lord'), $1 + 2$, $1 + 3$, and eventually $1 + 2 + 3$, in the textless version he compresses the process, moving from $1 + 2$ directly to the full combination of all three, cutting bars 73–87 and repairing the joins seamlessly.[7]

Samuel Butler, that arch-fanatic of all things Handelian, would have approved this wordless arrangement since, although he felt 'it would be hard to find a more satisfactory chorus even in the *Messiah*', he was worried by the repetition of 'the glory' and doubted the music was originally intended for these words: 'If these words had been measured, as it were, for a new suit instead of being, as I suppose, furnished with a good second-hand one, the word "the" would not have been tacked onto the "glory" which precedes it and made to belong to it rather than to the "glory" which follows.'[8]

The flowing semiquavers of the **Allegro (Mvt 3)** balance the blunter verbal rhythms of no. 2. The original image here was either the rushing Euphrates when the chorus opened the second act of *Belshazzar*, or the fluttering of leaves when it was part of the earlier cantata *Fronda leggiera e mobile* HWV 186. Maybe when it comes to pictorialism and symbolism we are more precious than Handel himself?

The **Largo (Mvt 4)** pits the oboes against the tutti (with one bar of bassoons *soli*), the contrast enhanced by Handel's specific markings of 'p' and 'f'. The small unit opening exchanges $(2 + 2)$ grow towards an exceptionally extended rising phrase over twelve bars without internal division. It opens with a backwards look, borrowing its first eight bars from the 3/8 aria 'S'io dir potessi' in *Ottone* (1722), which also has careful original dynamic markings, though the sublime rising scale is unique to the concerto version.

The strings again set the background motion for **Mvt 5, A tempo ordinario**, with more flowing violin semiquavers, this time as the canvas against which wind exclamations (both bands in unison) replace the chorus's cries of 'Lucky omens, bless our rites' from *Semele*. Handel takes only the first thirty-seven bars of the chorus, and then, at a cadence in the dominant, adds an Adagio confirming this conclusion and preparing the fugal entry of **Mvt 6, Alla breve moderato**. This is the later part of 'Lucky omens' (bars 48–109) with the text of 'Attend the pair' orchestrated without antiphony or separation of groups, the whole ensemble presenting unadapted four-part writing.

The **Minuet (Mvt 7)** also employs one unified group, and again, Handel dipped into his library: this is based on the bass aria 'Non t'inganni' from *Lotario* (1729) in F, itself remodelled as 'Thrice happy the monarch' in *Alexander Balus* (1747) in B flat; both were aggressive arias marked Allegro –.the rising semiquaver patterns there illustrate the word 'ottenga', to reach, rise, achieve, or in 1747 to 'defend with arms'. In the manuscript we can trace some of Handel's subtle changes of mind – his first 'Menuet' is altered to 'Minuet' and 'Allegro' is deleted, for example – suggesting that both formality and belligerence are being avoided. The movement is now almost seventy bars of gentle reflection on the accumulated catch-phrases of a lifetime extended by a system of variation that C. P. E. Bach was soon to utilise in his 'veränderte Reprisen' – the quirky recasting of small units. The predictable four-bar

Ex. 5.3

units of the *Lotario* aria (it is almost nothing but) are broken by three-bar phrases, and he uses the motto syncopation of quaver–crotchet more frequently but less monotonously than in *Lotario*. The pedal points (not normally a feature of dance movements except for rural pictorialism) still support rising semiquavers above them, but with the patterning less randomly varied. The whole apparently self-generating expression culminates in a rising scale made deliberately obvious by its rhythmic pattern repeated identically over seven bars, with ostentatiously no variation at all (see Ex. 5.3) – it would be hard to find a cooler statement of Handel's faith in his personal constructional skills, proving how much more can now be done with less subterfuge.

## *Concerto* HWV 333 (*Alexander Balus*, 1748)

If Smith had titled this concerto, it would have had to have been 'Concerto made from Airs and Choruses'. Handel again casts wide for his sources, drawing cavalierly from his earliest oratorio *Esther* and the even earlier *Ode for the Birthday of Queen Anne*, the most recent celebratory *Occasional Oratorio*, and the still little-heard *Messiah*. It is a measure of the consistency of his style over nearly thirty years that these components mesh so readily, and of his endless curiosity of mind that he could so completely re-assess them. The work was probably given as the added attraction for *Alexander Balus* at the Theatre Royal, Covent Garden on 23 March 1748.

The monumental three-way dialogue of the opening **Pomposo**, with harmonies ricocheting off the block orchestral chords in imperious dotted patterns from *coro* to *coro*, and rapid tirades linking them, provided a magnificent build-up to the entry of the counter-tenor Israelite in scene V of *Esther* announcing 'Jehovah crown'd with glory bright'. Given such trappings the solo is invested with more than the mere notes could achieve. The originality of Handel in pulling off this transformation is not only his being aware that the horn *could* do this but realising that no composer had previously *asked* it to. And only Handel could have seen the importance of a very small nuance, extending the horn cadence with a half-bar trill, which is not in the original; the following tirades are thus displaced by a half-bar, but the monumentality of the wordless statement is much enhanced.

**Mvt 2, Allegro** is the first section of the *Esther* chorus 'He comes to end our woes' which followed in the oratorio, tightened up by cutting the final three bars of horn fanfares. Construction and figuration are very similar to Mvt 2 of the *Concerto in Judas Maccabeus*, opening with fanfare figures for the horns of *Coro 1*, but quickly opting for the familiar 'battle' figuration (bars 31–2) ♩ ♫ ♫ ♩ which we have seen in similar circumstances (and key, and scoring) in WM3 – and which Handel will reach for yet again in *Fireworks Music* – and a straightforward instrumental version of the marcato theme 'to end our woes' (bar 39).

**A tempo giusto (Mvt 3)**; in the first word-book of *Messiah* this number, 'Lift up your heads' (no. 33), was described as 'Semichorus',[9] indicating a division between upper and lower voices for the question-and-answer form, with the altos rather awkwardly shared by both camps. At bar 34 this was abandoned for a single ensemble unified in singing 'He is the King of Glory'. In the instrumental version the moment of unification (bar 32) is adapted in favour of a close stretto between the *due cori*, the strings maintaining the progress of the original, but the winds doubling them in alternation with some fine independent bassoon writing. A small but typically Handelian ornamental figure is added to the repeated quaver figure ('The Lord of Hosts') from bar 61 to maintain the intensity which verbal momentum provided before (see Ex. 5.4).

In the vexed question of upbeats both here and in the *Messiah* version, 'tempo giusto' is surely meant to apply to the notated rhythms. Certainly Ernest Irving (see p. 124) believed that in principle such variety was intended by Handel. There is notable ingenuity of compression: bars

Ex. 5.4

13–18 of the original become 13–15 here, and 19–29 become 16–25, since they no longer support a verbal text, but the polychoral effect is increased. Note that neither in *Messiah* nor here does Handel propose an 'Adagio' for the cadential bars; a literal 'tempo giusto' to the end seems prescribed, since the note values are already greatly lengthened.

The chorus in slow siciliano rhythm 'Ye sons of Israel, mourn' is transcribed at full length as the **Largo (Mvt 4)**; the great choral exclamations of bars 11 and 12 are no less effective set for the combined winds against the unchanging string rhythms, and the horn parts can be seen in the manuscript to be a brilliant after-thought.

The **Allegro ma non troppo (Mvt 5)** is written 'upon a ground bass', a very English conceit that would have appealed to any elderly admirers of Purcell still around. In its much earlier incarnation in the *Ode for the Birthday of Queen Anne* (1713) the homage must have been deliberate, although this arrangement is based on the same ostinato that Handel had used for the chorus 'Thro' the nations he shall be next in dignity' in the later version of *Esther*. The four horns carry the lion's share of the drama, including their opening four bars of antiphonal challenges which Handel devised for this occasion and which act as an important landmark some ninety bars later; he was clearly aware of the dangers of protracted large-scale writing without a text to give sign-posts to the form.

The final **A tempo ordinario (Mvt 6)** draws on 'God found them guilty', the Act 1 finale of the recent *Occasional Oratorio*. Handel decided that the deliberate old-style seriousness of the original required its text to justify both length and speed; for the new context he increased the Andante marking to 'a tempo ordinario'; but after adapting the whole sixty-three bars of chorus to the new medium, he realised it was still unsustainable, slimmed it down to forty-seven bars, and then, in a brilliant change of texture, inserted virtuoso semiquaver passage-work for two solo oboes at the three major cadences (dominant, subdominant and relative minor) in the original fugue (bars 11, 20 and preceding bar

30 of the vocal version). In this concerto the solos are shared between both first oboes, supported by the one continuo line marked '*Violonc. et Contra B.*' – with, one assumes, the composer at the keyboard. Eventually the piece weighed in at ninety bars, but with the insertion of forty bars of substantial and developed new-style concerto element its wordless form was now justified. This is 'grouting' with a vengeance and certainly gives no evidence of a 'technique verging on laziness'.

The *Concerti a due cori* have been neglected, perhaps for their awkward scoring requirements, or perhaps because they demand a virtuosity far greater than either *Water Music* or *Fireworks Music*. They are not to be compared to his normal concertos or concerti grossi, forms he must by now have realised he had effectively exhausted. They show a sense of affirmation free from bombast, a welcome relief from the militaristic posturing required by the oratorios. The craftsmanship remains impeccable and at very least the result is shapely and varied interval music. But these pieces are additionally important as indicators that Handel was guilty neither of standing still nor of neglecting newer styles. His new focus on the sheer virtuosity of his players and the massive 'choral' setting he provided for exercising their instrumental skills sets them apart from anything else produced at this period. There is little to compare them with orchestrally, apart from the early attempts at the *sinfonia concertante* and Haydn's early symphonies with multiple solos, until Bartók.

Two further 'Concertos for Orchestra' (HWV 335a and b) had been on Handel's desk before the three *due cori* pieces were constructed. Strictly speaking, they are two versions of one concerto, in D and F, related rather as the alternate versions of WM11 and 12 are to their D major versions. Both call for four horns and 335a adds two trumpets and timpani. These concertos are usually mentioned for their opening movement, which they share with *Fireworks Music*, but their scoring shows that Handel had been pursuing a type of 'concerto for orchestra' for oratorio use for some time. HWV 335a is a composite of organ concerto and concerto for orchestra, with a bass-line (Mvt 2) marked *Violon. / Org* and indications for 'Organo ad libitum' after that movement, and 335b is also marked *Vc. et Violoni / Org*. Both concertos have the 'fade-out' endings that Handel used for the end of an opera, but were equally useful if the concerto was designed to segue into the final act of an oratorio. (The insertion of preliminary music is one reason why the final acts of oratorios are always the shortest.)

Although in the second movement of the D major the two oboes and bassoon simply double the strings, in the first and last they are free to alternate and to combine forces with the horns in the *due cori* manner; the strings pursue an independent path throughout. The 'fugue' we will meet again in *Fireworks Music*; here the brass take no part in the fugal sections, and only venture to the dominant in the modulating passages. The final 3/4 Allegro ma non troppo (eighty-three bars in both versions) is related distantly to the E major Andante section of the Coronation Anthem *My Heart Is Inditing* (to the text 'Upon thy right hand did stand the Queen') with its upwards slides but with none of its dotted rhythms and its 'other-worldly' tonality of E major.

We have no information about whether one or both of these works was ever used in an oratorio, but before long the opening movement was to be resurrected for Handel's last and largest contribution to the public image of the Hanoverian court.

# 6

# Politics and peace

The Peace is signed between us, France, and Holland, but does not give the least joy; the stocks do not rise, and the merchants are unsatisfied . . . in short, there has not been the least symptom of public rejoicing; but the government is to give a magnificent firework.

(Horace Walpole to Horace Mann, 24 October 1748)

The *Musick for the Royal Fireworks* (a propaganda title – Handel simply called it *Ouverture*) was commissioned by a worried government to prop up an unpopular and very soon disregarded treaty. The royal mention was needed to deflect public scrutiny away from the ministers involved, and the political consequences of a propaganda failure might have been fatal to dreams of a future British Empire. Tens of thousands turned out to watch this most lavish and hyped public show of the eighteenth century, yet no account, public or private, has so far come to light which describes or comments on Handel's music.

The Treaty of Aix-la-Chapelle (present-day Aachen) was devised to bring to an end the War of Austrian Succession, a squabble for colonial power largely played out between England and France – in America the conflict is still referred to as 'King George's War'. The various signatories were George II, the Empress Maria Theresia, Louis XV of France, Charles Emanuel III of Sardinia, Ferdinand VI of Spain, Francis III of Modena, the United Provinces of the Low Countries and the Republic of Genoa. Many of its conditions were unfavourable to Britain: by agreeing to return to the *status quo ante bellum*, the fortress of Louisbourg on Cape Breton Island, Nova Scotia, was to be returned to France, upsetting hard-fought British plans for greater colonial activity in America, and Gibraltar (essential to the Navy's forays towards Africa) was also to be relinquished. On the other hand, it gave Madras back to the British, and

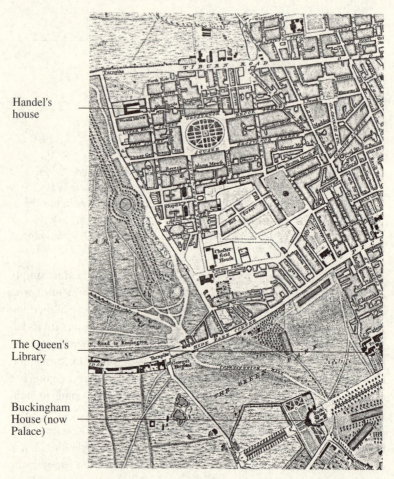

Handel's house

The Queen's Library

Buckingham House (now Palace)

Plate 4   *A plan of the cities of London and Westminster and borough of Southwark*, 1749/50, published by John Pine and John Tinney, after John Roque

at the same time confirmed the succession of the House of Hanover in Great Britain, so that dynastically as well as commercially, the King could be persuaded to see it as a triumph. But his ministers had private doubts: Lord Sandwich, the British representative at the signing, wrote to the Duke of Bedford 'I am afraid we should be thought bad legislators should we sign a definitive treaty with France, give up Cape Breton to them, and leave Flanders in their hands', and warring pamphlets were

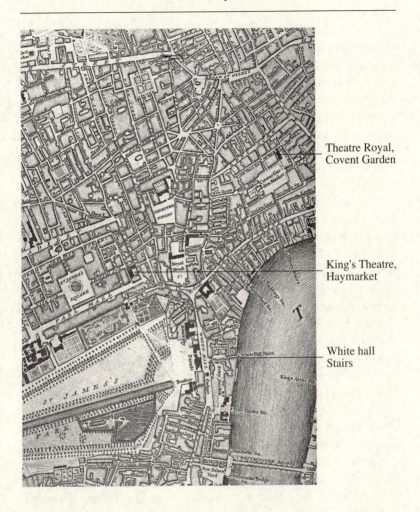

Theatre Royal,
Covent Garden

King's Theatre,
Haymarket

White hall
Stairs

quick to repeat these doubts in print. One cynically explained 'The Advantages of the Difinitive [*sic*] Treaty to the People of Great Britain Demonstrated' (London, 1749), another exposed a 'National Prejudice opposed to the national interest; candidly considered in the detention or yielding up Gibraltar and Cape Breton by the ensuing peace...' (London, 1748). Frankly, there was little to celebrate, as Walpole noted, and some dramatic spin-doctoring was called for to stimulate (or simulate) public approval.[1]

The first celebratory plans were sub-regal. In October 1748, with the Peace Preliminaries drawn up and awaiting ratification, *The Gentleman's Magazine* announced that 'fire-works are making by the Woolwich-warren engineers at the expence of 8000 £ [probably a misprint for £800] to be play'd off before the D. of Newcastle's house in Lincoln's Inn-field' (October 1748). But seeing the nation's disquiet at the less than honourable terms, what was first intended as a small-scale, aristocratic affair was now expanded and refocused on the King rather than the Parliamentarians who were coming under attack for giving away too much. Hence 'Royal' was essential to the title, and Handel was probably told as much.

The date was also postponed to April of the following year, to give time for grander preparations, extra spin, larger public attendance and, possibly, better weather. The site chosen was the fashionable upper part of St James's Park, recently improved at the Queen's instigation, which was becoming separately known as Green Park. It was a short walk from Buckingham House (not yet Palace) and was overlooked by the Queen's Library, designed by William Kent, and demolished in the nineteenth century. From the Library the progress on the building of the 'Machine' could be followed during the winter months.

Ground was broken in early November and a military fence ('a double row of chevaux de frize') guarded by musketeers erected to prevent public access (see Plate 6, p. 81 below). Some were already bored. Lady Jane Coke, as early as December 1748, wrote that she was 'tired of hearing about the fireworks', fearing that they would 'damage the houses in St. James' Street and break the windows in the Queen's Library'.

Engravings of the promised structure and descriptions of 'the *intended* Fireworks' were printed, most of them unofficial, and the increased man-power of the music was announced in *The London Magazine*, 14 January 1749:

> The band of musick that is to perform at the fire-works in the green-park, is to consist of 40 trumpets, 20 French horns, 16 hautboys, 16 bassoons, 8 pair of kettle-drums, 12 side-drums, a proper number of flutes and fifes; with 100 cannon to go off singly at intervals, with the musick. See the VIEW of the fire-works in our Magazine for December last.

In the caption to that engraving Handel's name had been mentioned for the first time: 'a Band of a Hundred Musicians are to play before y$^e$

Fire works begin, the Musick for w$^{ch}$ is to be compos'd by M$^{r.}$ Handel', from which we might assume that the composer was aware of the proposed instrumentation and had agreed to write for it. However, later developments suggest this may have been wishful thinking.

Postponement also gave time for increased public criticism. Some complained of the cost of the 'Machine' ('One mite remains, our Wealth to *War* a prey / To *Peace*, for joy, we give that mite away'); the more puritanical recommended 'severe reflection on the cause of its being erected, and the evil resulting from it'; and the sternest religious opponents drew the worst of comparisons 'On seeing the workmen employ'd upon the preparations for the fireworks on SUNDAY':

> . . . From her once fav'rite isle *Religion's* fled
> And we again in heathen footsteps tread:
> Like the poor *Persians*, we no more aspire,
> Sunk from the God of heav'n to serve the God of fire.[2]

These and similar condemnations of 'The *Funeral-Pile* of our *departed Glory*' resonate with our more recent public despair over the Millennium Dome. Like the Dome, the fireworks were irretrievably connected with the establishment and political success, and tried to bridge the gap to public favour; just as *Water Music* helped keep the King's image sweet, so *Fireworks Music* celebrated the national benefit from the power this generated. Unlike the Dome, however, the fireworks were run as a successful commercial enterprise as well as a symbol of monarchical power.[3] The prudent George would surely have been pleased equally by both.

Similar if smaller displays were no novelty to the House of Hanover. A 'Royal Fire-work' had been given on the Thames at Whitehall in 1713 after the peace of Utrecht. The more recent marriage of the Prince of Wales had been celebrated with *Atalanta*, for which Handel contributed to an ending of 'Illuminations and Bonfires, accompanied by loud Instrumental Musick'; this noisy number enjoyed a separate popularity as 'the Fire Musick'.

Significantly more attention had been given after the Utrecht and Dettingen successes to the religious justification of the victories, with elaborate church anthems and much ritual. Although there was to have been an elaborate service in St Paul's the day before the fireworks (originally the 7th), similar to the post-Dettingen celebrations, this was suddenly cancelled and in the end the various parties (Court, Lord Mayor, House of

Plate 5   Ticket for the Royal Fireworks, 1749

Commons and the Lords) all went to different churches. The King attended the Chapel Royal on the 25th, where Handel's *Peace Anthem* was given (mostly based on old material),[4] but drew little comment.

This time, it seems, the public message was that détente had been arranged with royal rather than divine assistance. On the 'Machine' the King's effigy was surrounded by exclusively mythological deities, and the Latin inscriptions were fully employed praising 'The Establisher of our Tranquillity, The Father of his People . . .' and especially 'The happy Re-establishment of Commerce'. Most brazenly, the engraved ticket produced for a seat in the grandstands showed not fireworks but a mondial globe depicting the trade routes to the Americas and Africa. The goddess of Peace, waving an olive branch, is perched on a disgruntled lion, with a garnishing of navigational instruments, agricultural tools and (charmingly) the muses of painting and music – the whole confection very honestly supported on two cannon (Plate 5).

Visual symbolism, in fact, was the real significance of the show. Fireworks would be the focus for a single evening, but the Machine with its emblems stood (and was widely publicised) for several months. Such a scheme was no novelty, but part of a long-standing European tradition; Italian and German 'pleasure fires' had been the delight of European courts since the sixteenth century.[5]

The German style was a *Feuerwerkschloss* or a *Denkmalsfeuerwerk* which celebrated a royal birth, marriage or appointment with a background construction in front of which the fireworks were set, while the Italian speciality (England's choice) was the *girandola*, a temple or monument construction with the fireworks concealed within. A third variety, the *Naumachia*, was a composite water and fire show, based round a *Feuerwerkschiff*, as in the regular celebrations of St John Nepomuk on the Vltava in Prague, or the canal displays at Versailles. Such pyrotechnical extravaganzas peaked in the 1690s, after which more literary and symbolic shows were preferred, the province of theatre designers rather than architects. Sometimes they would be a *drama di fuoco* with a plot, pantomime, jousting and several 'acts', sometimes simply a symbolic play of firepower at night. In all cases, the symbolism, the architecture, the allegorical statues and the Latin exhortations assumed greater and loftier pretensions in the eighteenth century.

The Green Park 'Machine' was thus a theatrical contrivance, its design and operation in the hands of technicians imported from France and Italy. The Chevalier Servandoni (originally Jean-Nicholas Servan), designer of the Machine, was, according to Diderot, 'grand machiniste, grand architect, bon peintre et sublime décorateur'. He had previously worked for the King's Theatre as a scene painter for Handel's operas during the 1720s, and shortly after the Fireworks he was involved in providing what was promised to be 'such magnificence of scenery as was never exhibited in Britain before' for Smollett's *Alceste*; Handel supplied the music, but the show was aborted. Servandoni also had a long history of designing *son et lumière* spectacles and firework displays in Paris from the celebration at the birth of the Dauphin in 1729 to the peace celebrations of 1749 just two months earlier, when his construction was trashed by demonstrators (see below, p. 87). For London he devised 'a magnificent Doric Temple' in best *trompe-l'œil* style, for what was grandly termed the 'solemnization of the General Peace':

Tho' the materials were only wood, and canvas whitewash'd and siz'd, it appeared in great elegance, like a temple of fine stone, with a balustrade on the top, except in the center [*sic*], where instead of a pediment, it went strait up in order to receive some pictures and the king's arms, to the top of which it was 114 foot high, and being adorned with statues and other figures, festoons of flowers, and other lustres, gave great delight to the beholders, which were innumerable. From this temple, which was 144 feet in length, extended, by 5 arches of a side two low wings, north and south, at the end of each a pavilion, the whole length being 410 feet. The several prints published, not excepting that by authority, of this structure, did not agree with the appearance on the night of performance.[6]

The official booklet itemises the 'Inscriptions, Statues, Allegorical Pictures, *&c.*' giving translations of all the Latin sentiments and descriptions of the bas-relief paintings of the King ('twenty-eight Feet by ten') and assorted deities, which were to turn into illuminated panels: 'The PICTURES in the Front of the Machine are eighteen, each painted double: They at first appear as Marble Basso Relievos, and after the Firework is played off they are removed by Machinery, and discover Pictures representing the same Subject in Colours, which are rendered transparent by a great Number of Lampions.'

This art of 'illumination from within' was also imported from the Italian theatre. However ephemeral the actual fireworks, the important transparencies of metaphorical figures and mythological scenes would be visible for hours. Handel would have been familiar with the technique from the elaborate settings for *La Resurrezione* in Rome in 1708 where a large 'carta trasparente' was backlit by seventy light-pans.[7]

Significantly, the *Description* notes: 'The following PICTURES are not rendered transparent, *viz.* The *Genii* of PEACE burning Heaps of Arms on each End of the Machine . . .' Britain was at war again within seven years.

The actual fireworks were devised and controlled by Gaetano Ruggieri and Giuseppe Sarti, both from Bologna. The Ruggieri family represents one of the longest-surviving dynasties in the pyrotechnical trade; they later fired the celebrations for the French Revolution, and were still around to supervise the display in New York Harbour when the Statue of Liberty was re-dedicated in 1986. Working in collaboration with the Royal Laboratory at Woolwich, they planned for an estimated 10,000 rockets and other devices to be let off, culminating in the grand Sun on

A. A Perspective View of the Building for the Fireworks in the Green Park; taken from the Reservoir.

Printed according to Act of Parliament & Sold by T. Bowles in St Pauls Church yard. John Bowles & Son at the Black Horse in Cornhill & R. Sayer opposite Fetter Lane, Fleet Street.

Plate 6  *A Perspective View of the Building for the Fireworks in the Green Park*, published by P. Brookes

the top of the Machine, supposed to burn for five hours with 'VIVAT REX' in its centre in 'bright Fire'.

In charge of this operation and its volatile crew were the Duke of Montagu, Master General of the Ordnance and, on the site, the fussy Charles Frederick, grandly titled 'Comptroller of His Majesty's Fireworks as well as for War as for Triumph'. Nervousness meant that throughout the building process Frederick was 'in the Green Park from 8 in the morning till 4 in the afternoon, has an office built there for him. The rest of the day he gives audiences and worries his spirits and his person till 'tis reduced to a shadow.'[8]

> *Horace Walpole to Henry Seymour Conway (6 October 1748)*
> Charles Frederick has turned all his virtu into fireworks, and, by his influence at the Ordnance, has prepared such a spectacle for the proclamation of the Peace as is to surpass all its predecessors of bouncing memory. It is to open with a concert of fifteen hundred hands, and conclude with so many hundred thousand crackers all set to music, that all the men killed in the war are to be wakened with the crash, as if it was the day of judgement, and fall a-dancing, like the troops in the *Rehearsal*. I wish you could see him making squibs of his papillotes, and bronzed over with a patina of gunpowder, and talking himself still hoarser on the superiority that his firework will have over the Roman *naumachia*.

One of Frederick's many headaches was attempting to control the pre-publicity. Servandoni had independently advertised his own publication on the fireworks 'without consulting the Duke of Montagu, the Controller Mr Frederick or anybody' and plagued the Duke 'almost every day', and there was a rash of other freelance and fanciful engravings purporting to represent 'the design'. In January the Office of Ordnance advised the public that 'Whereas several inaccurate and faulty prints of the edifice . . . have been lately published, and others are advertised, by persons neither sufficiently instructed or properly authorised . . . correct plans, profiles and elevations of the edifice, and a compleat view of the fireworks, together with a full explanation of the whole, will be published . . .'

In addition to the official *Description of the machine for the fireworks, with all its ornaments, and a detail of the manner in which they are to be exhibited in St. James's Park*, George Vertue was commissioned to produce twenty-five commemorative plates of the Machine and its decorations, to demonstrate, as he explains, that the enterprise was 'equal to such works done beyond [the] seas especially the noble illuminations & fireworks at Paris on the marriage of the Infanta of Spain 1738'. However, what with the intrigues of rival engravers, pirate publications and public saturation, in the end only one of his plates appeared.[9]

Handel's inclusion in the scheme, if not actually an afterthought, appears to have been rather delayed. This may have been the fault of his own diary rather than official procrastination, and probably some bargaining went on over what was musically possible in terms of the massed military instruments already promised. There were also more immediate engagements; his oratorio season at Covent Garden ran from 10 February to 23 March, where he presented, rehearsed and directed five different works. In addition he had to cope with the arrival of the soprano Frasi, write and direct the *Anthem on the Peace* and the Te Deum and work on the libretto for *Theodora*, which he planned to compose during July. His impatience with bureaucracy is easily understandable and comes across vividly in the letters of those officials who had the job of dealing with him. Mr Frederick was highly-strung and unsympathetic, but the Duke of Montagu had been a director of the early Royal Academy opera company in 1719 and Handel had rehearsed at Montagu House in Great Russell Street (it would later become the British Museum); Montagu at least must have been aware of the obstinacy of the man with whom he was dealing, though it is hard to sense it through his unique way with English.

From the first surviving letter, it appears they had already encountered problems persuading Handel to hold a public rehearsal in Vauxhall Gardens, with the intended pay-off that Jonathan Tyers, the Master of Vauxhall, would in return lend all his lanterns and lamps, plus thirty men, to illuminate the giant transparencies in Green Park.

*Duke of Montagu to Charles Frederick (28 March 1749)*

I don't see any kind of objection to the rehersal of the musick at Voxhall being advertised, and when that is done, if any questions are asked how it comes to be there, the true reason must be given.

I think Hendel now proposes to have but 12 trumpets and 12 French horns; at first there was to have been sixteen of each, and I remember I told the King so, who, at that time, objected to their being any musick; but, when I told him the quantity and number of martial musick there was to be, he was better satisfied, and said he hoped there would be no fidles. Now Hendel proposes to lessen the nomber of trumpets, &c, and to have violeens. I don't at all doubt but when the King hears it he will be very much displeased. If the thing war to be in such a manner as certainly to please the King, it ought to consist of no kind of instruments but martial instruments. Any other I am sure will put him out of humour, therefore I am shure it behoves Hendel to have as many trumpets, and other martial instruments, as possible, tho he don't retrench the violins, which I think he shoud, tho I beleeve he will never be persuaded to do it. I mention this as I have very lately been told, from very good authority, that the King has, within this fortnight, expressed himself to this purpose.

Although it is always assumed that Handel did not want to rehearse in Vauxhall for logistical reasons – and surely the full band would not have fitted into the 'Music Box' – the fact that the event was to be publicly 'advertised' (and the Gardens to make a fine profit from tickets) may have been the true cause. Handel not only wanted the music new for the event, he had recently engaged to repeat *Fireworks Music* as part of a Foundling Hospital concert four weeks afterwards, and would not have wanted to lessen the pulling power of this charity matinee.

The scoring argument may perhaps be reduced to a conflict between professionals (Servandoni, Handel) and amateurs (Frederick, Montagu) in the business of dramatic and musical presentation. Starting from the musically obvious, we can easily surmise that Handel realised three important factors from the very beginning. First, the originally publicised 'military' forces could never have played together: forty trumpets against sixteen oboes could not have been contained in a single composition, since the brass would have entirely out-balanced the winds; more probably a series of marches contrasted with fanfares had been envisaged. Montagu reported that the next level proposed was sixteen trumpets and sixteen horns, and that these were further reduced to twelve of each, and finally nine. Perhaps the simplest explanation is that the number of extra military players who could read music was insufficient; army personnel (then as now) played from memory. Handel was simply biding his time as the figures decreased. In the second place, any work written for such an extraordinary band would have had no future after its premiere. Handel may have been reminded of this point by his publisher, John Walsh, but certainly the newly proposed benefit for the Foundling Hospital must have provoked the incorporation of the strings. Thirdly, Handel surely realised that no other local composer would, at this stage, be competent to provide the necessary score.

Years of experience with theatrical negotiations would have suggested to Handel that he allow Mr Frederick, clearly a musical innocent, a glimpse of the manuscript showing strings, and use that as leverage to reduce the unworkable numbers of brass. He would offer to eliminate the strings, which he well knew would have made no effect in Green Park anyway, in exchange for a manageable number of military instrumentalists who could read music. Meanwhile he continued to indicate in the score where string parts would be needed at the Foundling Hospital.

*Montagu to Frederick (9 April 1749)*

I think it would be proper if you woud write an other letter to Hendel, as from yourself, to know his absolute determination, and if he wont let us have his overture [Handel was clearly threatening to withhold the MS] we must get an other, and I think it woud be proper to inclose my letter [see following] to you in your letter to him, that he may know my centiments; but don't say I bid you send it to him.

The letter enclosed for forwarding seems, if anything, to be more abrasive (and curiously spelled) than the Duke's private message to Frederick:

Sunday, 9 April, 1749

Sir, – In answer to Mr. Hendel's letter to you (which by the stile of it I am shure is impossible to be of his indicting) I can say no more but this, that this morning at court the King did me the honor to talke to me conserning the fireworks, and in the course of the conversation his Majesty was pleased to aske me when Mr. Hendel's overture was to be rehersed; I told his Majesty I really coud not say anything conserning it from the difficulty Mr. Hendel made about it, for that the master of Voxhall, having offered to lend us all his lanterns, lamps, &c. to the value of seven hundred pounds, whereby we woud save just so much money to the office of Ordnance, besides thirty of his servants to assist in the illuminations, upon condition that Mr. Hendel's overture shoud be rehersed at Voxhall, Mr. Hendel has hetherto refused to let it be at Foxhall, which his Majesty seemed to think he was in the wrong of; and I am shure I think him extreamly so, and extreamly indifferent whether we have his overture or not, for it may very easily be suplyd by another, and

I shall have the satisfaction that his Majesty will know the reason why we have it not; therefore, as Mr. Hendel knows the reason, and the great benefit and saving it will be to the publick to have the rehersal at Voxhall, if he continues to express his zeal for his Majesty's service by doing what is so contrary to it, in not letting the rehersal be there, I shall intirely give over any further thoughts of his overture and shall take care to have an other.

The bickering probably subsided once the bureaucrats had put their minds to who exactly 'an other' composer might be. Such were the squabbles preceding the most elaborate display that eighteenth-century London would see, and Handel's last ceremonial composition for the House of Hanover.

## A French entr'acte

The French celebration of the same treaty is worth examining for a moment since it highlights the different approaches of two governments, and reveals one surprising similarity. While England was preparing what some thought a rather 'foreign' entertainment – a 'French' *ouverture*, written by an (ex-)German, the set designed and fireworks operated by Italians – on the other side of the Channel, the French government was facing similar difficulties with its citizens, equally displeased with their side of a poor treaty. Louis XV admitted as much by declaring that he had made peace 'en roi et non en marchand' and the catch-phrase of the day became 'bête comme la paix'.

France had lost almost all of Flanders, important footholds in America, and even had to agree to the humiliation of not fortifying Dunkirk. They, too, chose to focus on the majesty of the King (while minimising the presence of Madame de Pompadour who, it was known, had pressed for the peace). Throughout the state, celebrations of Louis' 'grandeur d'âme' were ordered; Lille put up a Temple to Peace, and in Reims, on 13 March 1749, the town hall was decked with effigies of King and Queen, patriotic inscriptions (this time in French) and supported by flambeaux, 'feu de joye' and fireworks; there was music 'des trompettes, des fifres, des hautbois, des tambours et des timbales' – all very similar to the English plans.

But the effect of the campaign was less successful. Where the English dissidents had limited their disapproval to libellous verses, the French public was less compliant; when the same Servandoni who designed the Green Park 'Machine' erected a similar 'très belle décoration' in February, the Marquis d'Argenson noted in his diary that 'the people, egged on by the opposition, had overthrown the decoration, broken it up and burnt it'.

Seeing such active dissatisfaction, Louis took steps to bolster his image in Paris; an opera and (later) a statue were ordered. Both, in a sense, represent more lasting versions of the English solution; the festivities for the dedication of the statue in Place de Louis XV (the present Place de la Concorde) in 1763 lasted three days, with full illuminations in the Tuileries, trumpets, drums and a 'serenade des symphonies par l'Académie Royale de Musique'. The opera *Naïs*, on the other hand, was given to the usual exclusive audience at l'Académie royale de musique, and was planned (at Mme de Pompadour's prompting) as a gesture of royal superiority in the face of a critical public. Described as 'Opéra pour la Paix', and a 'pastorale-héroïque', with words by Cahusac and music by Rameau, *Naïs* was overladen with symbolism.[10]

'L'Ouverture est un bruit de guerre qui peint les cris et les mouve-ments tumulteux des Titans et des Géants'; the enormous (and almost atonal) Prologue showing the struggles of the Titans and the Giants leads eventually into a chorus, 'Attaquons les cieux', as they storm the hea-vens. The Overture and Scene I alone fill seventy-three pages of modern score before an 'Entr'acte à la place de l'Ouverture' leads to the first of three acts of mythology in defence of the divine right of monarchs. Even Handel's public gestures seem slight beside this Goliath; but, as history showed forty years later, it was more politic to mollify the public than mock them.

Before returning to the London scene, however, it is worth quoting the opening of Rameau's 'Entracte in place of the overture'; in spite of their differences, it seems that the once opposing sides celebrated the same treaty with the same tune (see Ex. 6.1).

The similarity between this and Handel's *Réjouissance* is too marked to miss. Yet, although we know that Handel borrowed the motive, it was from an opera written thirty years earlier by Giovanni Porta (see Ex. 7.15, p. 117); since Rameau's opera opened only one day after *Fireworks Music* was rehearsed at Vauxhall Gardens, there can have been no connivance. So who is 'indebted' to whom? Or could all three composers have been drawing on a common military call?[11]

Ex. 6.1

Back in London, bickering resolved, there was a preliminary run-through of *Music for the Royal Fireworks* in Brook Street on 17 April.[12] Even if it involved the principals only and no timpani it could still have been a trial for the neighbours. This would have been the last time when alterations and scribbled instructions were added to the manuscript: full scores of instrumental pieces were not used for conducting.

Handel had evidently conceded the Vauxhall rehearsal which, after several changes of date, had finally been fixed for 21 April at 11 a.m. It attracted

> the brightest and most numerous Assembly ever known at Spring Gardens, Vauxhall . . . an audience of above 12000 persons (tickets 2s. 6d.). So great a resort occasioned such a stoppage on *London-Bridge*, that no carriage could pass for 3 hours; – The footmen were so numerous as to obstruct the passage, so that a Scuffle happen'd, in which some gentlemen were wounded. (*The Gentleman's Magazine*, April 1749, p. 185)

Normal entry to Vauxhall was a shilling; at the elevated rate of 2/6, 12,000 people, if the number were true, would have yielded a more than tidy profit for Jonathan Tyers of over £1500. But the figure is physically impossible; allowing for normal means of transport – foot, carriage, boat – it could have been 4,000 (or even a misprint for 1–2,000),[13] making this still a high-priced event. Westminster Bridge, so recently built, was already closed for subsidence repairs, making a traffic jam on the old London Bridge inevitable. A sarcastic letter in the *London Evening Post*, 1 November 1748, had suggested that the closed bridge be used for the firework display.[14]

The Royal Artillery Train again loaned Handel the timpani from the Tower, as they had for *Joshua*, but more surprising are the 'Eighteen Chambers' and thirty-six pounds of explosive delivered to Mr Frederick at Vauxhall.[15] Was this for incidental salutes to be added to the rehearsal, and, if so, may they in fact have been included within the composition, as one description states? ('After a grand Overture of Warlike Instruments, composed by Mr. *Handel*, in which eighteen small Cannon were fired . . .')

In spite of the (over-estimated) number of people at the public rehearsal, no description of Handel's music appears in any report of the event, either public or private. The same neglect has to be admitted for the actual show itself, where the numbers were even greater, but the music was still marginalised by the spectacle and its incidental disasters. Government Orders were issued that 'No Coach will be suffered to come into the Park after Seven O'clock in the evening' and (more prudently) 'No Flambeaux will be permitted to either coaches or chairs either in coming or going' (*General Advertiser*, 26 April). There was a sudden last-minute panic about overcrowding, allayed by some soothing figures in the *General Advertiser* (26 April):

> The following calculation of the dimensions of the Green Park has been made with all possible exactness and may serve to free many persons from the apprehension they may be under of there not being sufficient room to see the Fireworks. Half a mile square contains 774,400 square yards or 160 acres of land allowing 2 men to a yard; it will contain 1,540,000; allowing 3 to a yard it will contain 2,323,200. [At this date the total population of England and Wales was estimated at a little over 5 million.]

Advertisements appeared in the broadsheets for places in the galleries specially constructed both inside and outside the walls of the Park 'with covering to screen them from the Weather . . . Note, the highest Seat will not exceed nine Feet from the Ground.' These were for the well-to-do – the price of admission to the grandstand was 10/6, the same as a ticket to the Foundling Hospital *Messiah* the following year, or a box at Covent Garden (or a bottle of 'Dr Prossilly's Water for the Pox').

While it was still light, the King, his son 'Butcher' Cumberland and the court toured the 'Machine', and presented purses to the operatives. 'The whole Band of Musick (*which began to play soon after 6 o'clock*) perform'd at his Majesty's coming and going, and during his stay in the Machine.'[16]

At half an hour after eight, the works were begun by a single rocket from before the library, then the cannon within the chevaux de frize were fired; two rockets were afterwards discharg'd at the front camera of the inclosure, when 101 pieces of cannon placed on *Constitution-hill*, were discharged; after which a great number of rockets of different sorts, balloons, &c. were discharged, to surprising perfection. (*The Gentleman's Magazine*, p. 186)

The official *Description* shows that the display was planned in a series of eleven numbered scenes, each containing multiple firings and a set piece. The first scene alone involved:

120 Large Honorary Rockets.
96 Rockets in two Flights.
12 Mortars with Air Balloons.
12 Caduceus Rockets.
12 Girandole Rockets.

These fire together:

Two regulated Pieces, each consisting of Four Mutations, *viz.*

I. A large fixed Sun.
II. A Star of six Points, and between each Point a Ray.
III. A Star of ten Points.
IV. A compound Figure consisting of Points and Rays.
Four large double Wheels moved by four Fires.

Twenty Tourbillons.

*The Gentleman's Magazine*, noting 'all kinds of artists, affecting to make use of foreign words and phrases, rather than the common terms', obligingly translated the technical names:

HONORARY ROCKETS are the large rockets which are fired single . . . As all fireworks are considered as compliments to princes or great persons, the *French* have given the name of *Fusees d'honneur* to these rockets, which are constantly the beginning of every firework.
AIR BALLOONS, are hollow globes of paper filled with stars, &c. which are fired from mortars, and are contrived to burst when at their greatest altitude; some of the balloons fired on this occasion were remarkably fine.
CADUCEUS ROCKETS and GIRANDOLE ROCKETS. These had a circulating motion as they rose.

TOURBILLONS, are copied from the *Chinese*. They consist of a case of composition which rises not endways, like a rocket, but keeps horizontal in its ascent, and is contrived to turn round at the same time with an horizontal motion. – Some of these were very pleasing by their complicated movement.

However, the 'surprising' perfection did not last:

About half an Hour after Nine, in discharging some of the works from the Pavilion at the Left Wing of the Building, it set Fire to the same, and burnt with great *Fury*, so that that, and two of the Arches, were burnt to the Ground; and had not the Carpenters made a Breach by casting away two Arches, and removing the Timber, and for the Assistance of some Fire-Engines which were in Readiness, in all Probability the whole Fabric would have been consumed. Messengers were going to and from his Majesty all the Time of this Misfortune; and when it was brought under, a Present was made to the most diligent in stopping the Flames.

During the Fire, the grand Rockets and the Sun were discharged; but this Accident prevented the exhibiting some of the most considerable of the Fireworks.

About Eleven the whole Building was illuminated, and continued so until between Two and Three o'Clock. His Majesty and the Royal Family withdrew about Twelve. (*Description*, p. 8)

Three different eyewitnesses of differing position and partiality can be called on to bring the event to life: the dissenter in the park, the socialite from a private view and the noble 'dilettante' with the royal party in the Queen's Library.

John Byrom, the enigmatic Jacobite, was noted for his invention of a shorthand system used by the Wesleys and Horace Walpole, as well as for his poetry and hymns. He may also have filled a portfolio of disreputable roles of playboy, spy, cabalist and secret lover of Queen Caroline.[17] He seems to have visited the Fireworks alone, and naturally kept well away from the royals and more 'other great folks':

*John Byrom to his wife (27 April 1749)*
Green Park, 7 o'clock, Thursday night, before Squib Castle.
Walking about here to see sights I have retired to a stump of a tree to write a line to thee lest anything should happen to prevent me by and by . . .they are all mad with thanksgivings, Venetian jubilees, Italian fireworks, and German pageantry. I have before my eyes such a concourse of people as to be

sure I never have or shall see again, except we should have a Peace without a vowel. The building erected on this occasion is indeed extremely neat and pretty and grand to look at, and a world of fireworks placed in an order that promises a most amazing scene when it is to be in full display. His Majesty and other great folks have been walking to see the machinery before the Queen's Library; it is all railed about there, where the lords, ladies, commons, &c. are sat under scaffolding, and seem to be under confinement in comparison of us mobility, who enjoy the free air and walks here.

It has been a very hot day, but there is a dark overcast of cloudiness which may possibly turn to rain, which occasions some of better habits to think of retiring; and while I am now writing it spits a little and grows into a menacing appearance of rain, which, if it pass not over, will disappoint expectations. My intention, if it be fair, is to gain a post under one of the trees in St. James's Park, where the fireworks are in front, and where the tail of a rocket, if it should fall, cannot but be hindered by the branches from doing any mischief to them who are sheltered under them, so I shall now draw away to be ready for near shelter from either watery or fiery rain.

11 o'clock: all over, and somewhat in a hurry, by an accidental fire at one of the ends of the building, which, whether it be extinguished I know not, for I left it in an ambiguous condition that I might finish my letter, which otherwise I could not have done. I saw every fine show in front, and I believe no mischief was done by the rockets, though some pieces of above one pound and a half fell here and there – some the next tree to my station, and being on the watch I perceived one fall, and after a tug with four or five competitors I carried it off.

My dear, I shall be too late if I don't conclude; I am all of a sweat with a hasty walk for time to write; and now I'll take some refreshment and drink all your healths.[18]

Jemima, Marchioness Grey viewed the show from Lord Sundon's house in Cleveland Row, just north of St James's Palace, and sent a full report to her aunt.

*Lady Jemima Grey to Lady Mary Gregory (28 April 1749)*
I write Today my dear Aunt, because I imagine you will not be sorry to hear I am alive & well after the Fireworks. Whether you had raised to yourself so formidable an Idea of them as many had done, I don't know, or whether as being out of the way of all the Conversation they have furnished the Town with, you had thought less about them: but for Myself I own I expected the Day with some Terror in the Apprehension of what Mischiefs

such a sort of Spectacle & such Numbers of People assembled together might occasion, & I seriously thank God that it is happily over without any Accidents I have yet heard of. The Order with which it was conducted, & the regularity of the People in keeping to the Places allotted to them, were much greater than I expected; and the vast Numbers of them crowded together really made a fine Sight.

We went early to Ld. Sundon's to avoid the Mob we supposed would fill the Streets, & for two Hours before it was dark enough for the Fire-works to begin, sat much at our ease with only the Bishop's Family & two or three more Folks in the Room, to admire from his Windows in a charming Evening that most beautiful Building raised exactly before us, the large Area between us & it & around it quite free & empty, with only some People scatter'd about the Green that belonged to the Works, & the finest fine Ladies & Gem'men of the King's Party in the Library walking under our Windows for our Amusement: the Inclosure lined with Soldiers, & such a Concourse of People beyond as entirely hid the Ground: – Musick playing at proper Intervals to enliven us: – Can you imagine a gayer or finer Scene? – Yet this Crowd before one's Eyes was a painful as it was a great Sight, from the Notion of the many Mischiefs that might happen to them before they parted: – but when the Fireworks began my Fears were dispell'd by seeing the Regularity with which they went on, & no Appearance of Danger. – For about an Hour they succeeded literally speaking A Merveille; for the Number, the Sizes & various Forms of the Rockets were quite surprising, one Explosion particularly which they say was of Six Thousand was beyond all Imagination, & excepting to poor Mrs. Talbot who was frightened out of all her Wits (for it was not indeed a very Quiet Amusement) they were no less Beautiful. – But after about an Hour's Applause from the Spectators & Triumph in the Performers & Directors, one End Pavilion to the Building unluckily took Fire & spoilt the Show. It raised some Alarm you may be sure in the Fear of its spreading to the Rest, & it took up so many hands in putting it out or rather in preventing its gaining on (as it burnt down that single Piece) that the Firework was at a Stand, & what was let off after that was Irregular & in Confusion. The Illumination too which should have been done all at Once was performed but by Bits at a Time which quite spoilt the Effect, & when lighted it was not at last so pretty as an Opera-Scene. So that the whole Diversion was as Miss Talbot described it last Night, an Irregular Incompleat Whole consisting of several very Beautiful parts.

I could not help being concern'd last Night as a good English-Woman, that these Rejoicings we have made such a Rout with, which were to outdo those of all Other Nations, & that so many Foreigners were present at,

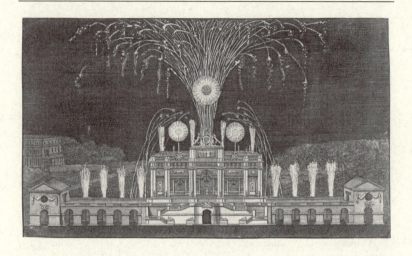

Plate 7    *A Night View of the Public Fireworks* (*The Universal Magazine*, 1749)

which have lost so much Time & cost so much Money (they say 15000£) should have failed in any Degree: but I was heartily thankful we all escaped so well from them.

I believe you hardly envy me my Diversion though it was certainly a fine One: – Nor can you have a Notion as you are quietly in the Country, what London has been this last Week! So brimfull, so busy, & so Idle, it never was known before! Everybody of Spirit & Genius (if not so Dull as you) crowding from the Country into Town to partake of the Diversions of the Time, & everybody in Town running about like Wild Things from one Place or One Sight to another: – even the Streets & Parks have been full every Day like a fair, of the Common People, gaping & staring at this great Building & all its Ornaments.

Masquerades & Fireworks are the only things that have filled our Brains for these ten Days. Of the First there was one at Ranelagh last Wednesday, & our Grand Subscription is for Monday: after that is over you may hear something more from me, but till then I am as Idle & simply busy as all my Neighbours . . .[19]

Horace Walpole was of the royal party watching from the Queen's Library (he refers to the burning north pavilion as being on the right); presumably the slow lighting of the illumination by Tyers' men was excused by them having been redeployed to deal with the fire.

*Horace Walpole to Horace Mann (3 May 1749)*

The next day were the fire-works, which by no means answered the expense, the length of preparation, and the expectation that had been raised; indeed, for a week before, the town was like a country fair, the streets filled from morning to night, scaffolds building wherever you could or could not see, and coaches arriving from every corner of the kingdom. This hurry and lively scene, with the sight of the immense crowd in the Park and on every house, the guards, and the machine itself, which was very beautiful, was all that was worth seeing. The rockets and whatever was thrown up into the air succeeded mighty well, but the wheels and all that was to compose the principal part, were pitiful and ill-conducted, with no changes of coloured fires and shapes: the illumination was mean, and lighted so slowly that scarce anybody had patience to wait the finishing; and then what contributed to the awkwardness of the whole, was the right pavilion catching fire, and being burned down in the middle of the show.[20]

The press naturally had feared for the worst and carried facetious advertisements for 'the famous Sieur Rocquet, Surgeon, just arrived from Paris necessary for all Gentlemen and Ladies that attend the Fireworks'. Accompanied by fifty assistants, he would be stationed 'as near to the several Scaffolds as can be done'; his various rates included the bleeding of a dead corpse, the removal of one or more limbs, or parts thereof, and the replacement of an eye, nose or teeth 'in the genteelest manner, and as now worn by persons of rank in *France*'.

In fact, the actual fireworks seem to have achieved only one direct hit, and that was extinguished decorously:

By one of the large Rockets darting strait forward into the Scaffold next the Library, it set fire to the Cloaths of a young Lady, which would soon have destroyed her, but some Persons present having the Presence of Mind to strip her Cloaths off immediately to her Stays and Petticoats, she escaped with only having her Face, Neck and Breast, a little scorched. (*Description*, p. 8)

The pessimists had a bad day: 'Fewer accidents happen'd on this occasion than were apprehended . . . A painter fell from the fire-works, and was killed on the spot. A shoemaker, who was in liquor, stooping to drink out of the great pond, fell in and was drowned . . .' Other than these casualties, and a bombardier who had blown off his arm while demonstrating the cannon to the King the previous day, many thousand people seem to have escaped damage. Even a tantrum from the designer, the last thing Mr Frederick needed, was quickly resolved: when the pavilion caught fire, Servandoni drew his sword on Frederick; he was disarmed and taken into custody, but released the following day after apologising.

The whole show lasted some nine hours, and in spite of all mishaps the sun, '32 feet in Diameter' and the literal high-light of the scheme, survived to fulfil expectations:

> As to the beautiful sun which you see represented on the top of the triumphal arch; it is composed of three circles of fiery fountains, each circle containing 180 cases of composition. Which fountains will be ranged like the spokes of a wheel with their mouths outermost. These fountains also will be placed alternately in the circle, *viz.* the mouths of the first circle opposite the intervals between the second, and the second between the third, and they being also mixed with steel dust, and fired at the same instant, will form a most brilliant glory resembling the streams of, or rays of light generally painted about the heads of saints, exceeding any thing of the kind ever seen before. (*The Universal Magazine of Knowledge and Pleasure*, 4 March, 1749, p. 139)

After the Fireworks day the celebrations continued with masquerades, balls and pleasure garden treats. A serenade entitled 'Peace in Europe' by an unknown composer was given in the Haymarket Theatre two days later (29 April) and there were repeats of fireworks at Cuper's Gardens on 17 May 'exceeding beautiful, and nearly representing the Royal ones'. By September this long-running show had become 'a curious and Magnificent Firework . . .'

Handel's music (or part of it) was heard again at the Foundling Hospital on 27 May, with 'violeens' (and presumably reduced winds) in a programme containing the music for the dedication of the Temple from *Solomon*, and the newly assembled 'Foundling Hospital Anthem'. The Prince and Princess of Wales attended, creating a balance of royal liaisons which must have pleased the composer. From the indications in the autograph, they may have heard a version of *Fireworks Music* that ended with the 'Allegro ma non troppo' of HWV 335a, omitting *La Réjouissance* and everything after it, presumably less apt for an indoor event.

For such a charitable performance Handel (who received a £50 honorarium) appears to have persuaded the players to give their services, since the minutes (31 May) state 'That Mr Handel be desired to return thanks of this Committee to the performers who voluntarily assisted him upon that occasion'. These were the first and last musicians to perform *Fireworks Music* with Handel in its indoor scoring.

# 7

# Music for the Royal Fireworks

It was from Handel that I learned that style consists in force of assertion. If you can say a thing with one stroke unanswerably you have style: if not, you are at best a *marchand de plaisir*: a decorative *littérateur*, or a musical confectioner, or a painter of fans with cupids and *cocottes*. Handel has this power . . . You may despise what you like; but you cannot contradict Handel.
(George Bernard Shaw, 'Causerie on Handel in England', 1913)[1]

The grandeur of the occasion, the scale of the architecture, the size of crowd expected, the expenditure on explosives – all were out of the ordinary, so it is clear that Handel's 'grand plan' must have put scale, both of composition and forces, as a priority: the epitome of positive assertion. But it was a peace celebration and a people's event, not an operatic battle scene for aristocrats; everyday prosperity and security presupposed the stability of the ruling house, and (at least the impression of) a large public support for the King was a salient objective. Servandoni supplied one of his largest designs in a strictly classical order, and Handel responded with the musical equivalent and his longest single instrumental movement.

The path towards *Fireworks Music* lay very directly via the *Concerti a due cori* and the two brass concertos associated with the 'military' oratorios. These works mark the peak of Handel's 'imperious' manner – large-scale musical statements of public optimism, showing how proficient he had become at focusing on (rather than creating) a public mood. It was also a manner he had tired of. After the military oratorios, he turned towards the more personal and introspective mode inspired by *Alexander Balus* and *Theodora* suggesting that, if the *Fireworks Music* commission had not arrived, he might at this point have abandoned the triumphalist style altogether.

Stravinsky pointed out that part of the art of being a successful composer was to 'be commissioned to write the piece you have just written'. It looks as though Handel was already prepared with the material for a grander and possibly final theatre piece when the *Fireworks Music* commission came along. Yet again he was essentially following a plan of 'writing for himself' in developing the 'concerto for orchestras' on his own terms; the peace celebration was the fortuitous catalyst.

Pope's description of Handel in Book IV of *The Dunciad* (1742) parades the received opinion that Handel was partial to the use of extreme forces (which in fact were more a feature of the revivals of his music after his death, although both *Esther* and *Deborah* were considered excessive in the 1730s): 'Mr Handel had introduced a great number of Hands and more variety of instruments into the Orchestra, and employed even Drums and Canon to make a fuller Chorus.'[2] 'Canon' probably meant the great kettle-drums which Handel borrowed from the Tower of London for *Saul*.

All Handel's previous military music had been small-scale marches for winds, a couple of wind 'arias' and the Overture for two clarinets and horn mentioned earlier (p. 63). The social status of these military instruments was well recognised: fife and side-drums for footguards, oboes for dragoons, trumpets and kettle-drums for horse guards. Trombones, associated with death and the supernatural, would usually be called on in instrumental music for a Dead March (as in *Saul*, or *Samson*). Handel added no instruments to *Fireworks Music* that he had not used before. Even the serpent and contra-bassoon on the bass line had precedents: a part for a serpent in both *Samson* and *Solomon* had been copied out,[3] and the 'Contra Bassone' (apparently singular) had already been proposed in *L'Allegro*. We have no way of telling whether the serpent (also apparently not available in multiples) was deleted from the score before or after the open-air performance. It is, in any case, not an assertive instrument – Thomas Hardy's inclusion of it in a music-gallery band in a small Dorset church (*Under the Greenwood Tree*) is more appropriate for its quite gentle tone.

All other instruments were utilised *en masse*, with no solos indicated anywhere in this score. Even the percussion, although reduced from the original '8 pair of kettle-drums, 12 side-drums' to three sets of timpani, would still suggest a proportional four or five side-drummers; 'better several

Plate 8 Autograph of *Music for the Royal Fireworks*

together than one alone' as Berlioz recommended.[4] No music was written out for the side-drums, nor had it been in the *Judas Maccabeus* March, but the players were trained in a variety of beats and signals such as the 'flam, drag, roofe, diddle, rowle' (described by Randle Holme in the *Academy of Armoury, c.* 1686). Of the specific rhythms, the rapid dactylic pattern ♫ ♫ ♩ was universally recognised as the signal for 'Fire!', hence its presence in all battle music. Whether the timpani (Handel spells it 'Tymp.') part was also open to elaboration is unclear; the notation is fully rhythmic as it stands, with only one 'tr' in the whole of *Fireworks Music* (bar 42 of the opening movement) and none in its earlier Concerto version. Handel's own part in this performance, like *Water Music*, is never made clear. Here, with no keyboard and no violin either, he was presumably either 'beating time' as he had done in the oratorios, or even leaving it to the band-masters.

The autograph of *Fireworks Music* (British Library RM 20.g.7) graphically shows Handel's various on-the-run solutions, nowhere more clearly than with the much-disputed string parts. He began adding indications for string doubling in the middle of *La Réjouissance* (possibly the moment when the Foundling Hospital performance was first mooted) then adapted the earlier movements by adding marginal instructions, but possibly not until after the Green Park celebrations. Apart from his normal compositional corrections, the manuscript shows two levels of erasure. Some markings are firmly crossed out and now quite illegible, but other parts are very lightly hatched, apparently to leave them legible for another occasion. Those firmly erased were, it seems, needed only for the open-air performance (the 'bruit de guerre' and the 'et serpent' for example), whereas the added indications for strings were lightly hatched so that they could be included in the Foundling Hospital parts and were still legible to Walsh's engraver (the parts were advertised as in print by 2 June). *Walsh* did not attempt a viola part (*Arnold* was the first to do so) since Handel's hasty 'Viola colla Bassi tutti' is not a water-tight instruction, and when asked to double Oboe III or Trumpet III questions of tessitura arise.

A first investigation of the broad and benign melody that opens the **Overture** might convince the listener that Handel had ingeniously decided to round off his orchestral career by making a direct adaptation of his early *Water Music* Hornpipe – using the same notes in almost the same order, with only a change of rhythmic patterns to achieve solemn grandeur rather than vigorous dance (see Ex. 7.1).

Ex. 7.1

Ex. 7.2

Much might be read into this, except that the idea started life before either of these works, as a keyboard *Aria with 24 variation*s by Johann Philipp Krieger (1649–1725), the Capellmeister in Weissenfels, where Handel was brought up. The piece was never published, but may have been one of the manuscript pieces in Handel's lost keyboard book described on p. 54 (see Ex. 7.2).

Handel had recourse to this fragment, which obviously held special attraction for him, five times in his life, each version making different decisions of detail and 'grand plan' and each a different length: in 1737 in *Berenice* for a Sinfonia of nineteen bars; the two brass concerto versions, thirty-eight bars (HWV 335a in D major) and thirty-nine bars (HWV 335b in F major) respectively; the opening of *Fireworks Music* (forty-five bars); and finally as an Ouverture in the 1759 version of *Solomon* (seventeen bars).

In *Berenice* (1737) Handel moved it from B flat to the key of C. There is no tempo marking but a certain anxiety is suggested by the fast-moving harmonic pulse from the end of bar 2 onwards, with imitations in all parts rather in the manner of the early, busy Allemande; the modulation to the dominant also comes quickly, by bar 6 (Ex. 7.3).

Once Handel had noted the potential of this theme for brass instruments (the outline fits the available notes of natural brass instruments very neatly, as the analogy with WM12 demonstrates), he moved it to the appropriate keys (D for trumpets, F for horns). Small experiments with canon, the rhythm of bar 2 and early on an ornamental device to remove a banal repetition in the second bar of tutti in all three works shows where

Ex. 7.3

Ex. 7.4

he felt the basic outline had a weakness, but for the larger canvas, he pointedly waits until bar 18 of *Fireworks Music* before employing this nuance (Ex. 7.4).

Within the confines allowed by the brass instruments Handel also pursued several alternative harmonisations of the first bars (Ex. 7.5).

Ten years after *Fireworks Music*, Handel reused its opening bars in a strangely retrograde remake as the *Ouverture* to open the last act of a drastically altered (some would say vandalised) *Solomon*. It is difficult to be sure whether this was totally Handel's doing or the work of

Ex. 7.5

J. C. Smith and the Brook Street 'factory'. Perhaps Handel, like Mendelssohn, suffered from *Revisionskrankheit* and liked the process so much he did not know when to leave a good thing alone. We find yet another harmonisation of the first eight bars and a repeat with trumpets added (but lacking that inspired trumpet top B on the modulation in bar 12 of *Fireworks Music*) before it cadences in the dominant to lead into the following Chorus. The five different transformations of one simple theme produce a synoptic sensation rather akin to reading the same Biblical verse in five different translations (Ex. 7.6).

The original markings at the head of *Fireworks Music*, 'Concerto' and 'Adagio', are both erased, suggesting that Handel may have started work on the first page of another oratorio concerto before the commission for a fireworks overture arrived. The cancelling of the tempo marking is also a reminder that this is no longer a typical dotted French overture, but more a slow march in the 'speaking' style of Lully or Purcell and the earlier English composers. Nevertheless, French allusions remain in all the movement titles, and the falling cadence in bar 3 looks like a written-out *tierce coulée*. Was Handel expecting *notes inégales* and altered rhythms throughout? In bars 31–7 this would seem very unsuitable, and yet bar 39 gives the falling cadence with a dotted rhythm in all parts (Ex. 7.7).

Ex. 7.6

Tierce coulé

Ex. 7.7

In all three of these versions the melodic opening is displaced by a half-bar; Handel supplies the down-beat with an opening bass-note rather as he did for the start of the 'Harmonious Blacksmith' variations, or the full chord that opens WM11. This may have been for orchestral safety, or to

Ex. 7.8

signal the introduction of a quotation, but the effect of such a gathering note in *Fireworks Music* enhances the hymn-like, congregational quality of the homophony. It is uncertain whether the metrical layout of such pieces was very meaningful to Handel; he would frequently add or subtract half a bar during 'surgery' (making life very complicated for his copyists) and thus change the whole metrical pattern of the piece. The nuanced suggestion of a hymn tune (like his Wesleyan settings) or psalm chant is well calculated to appeal to his broad audience: natural simplicity and 'common touch' first, expertise and ingenuity later. In fact, for the connoisseur, Handel cleverly ensures that every continuation grows organically from these opening bars, the only 'new' melodic motive (bar 31) deriving from the bass-line of bar 3 (Ex. 7.8).

Two architectural metaphors are suggested here. First, the reflection of the Machine itself in the arch-form of the seven-bar span of melody, firmly based at either end in D major. Even when the modulation to the dominant is inevitable, Handel prolongs the number of bars he uses, to make a convincingly epic moment of royal arrival compared with the mobility of the *Berenice* version and the Concerto 335a. Secondly, there is the heightened sense of effortless grandeur achieved by excising superfluous bars in the movement, just as removing columnar support from a great hall impels admiration for the science of building. Such contractions are visible in the manuscript between bars 19 and 20 and again between bars 31 and 32 where two bars were removed; the original long version was as shown in Ex. 7.9 – the small notes in the example showing Handel's reworking to smooth over the cut.

Although Handel is clearly working directly from the material assembled in 335a, the eventual construct grows to forty-six bars with two important differences: more small-scale antiphonal fanfares and, most tellingly, the addition of a new walking bass for bars 31–5 which adds both expansiveness and a sense of direction missing in 335a. A sense of scale as well as security is thus transmitted early on in the piece. Handel knew well how to imply a long structure at the outset of a work:

Ex. 7.9a

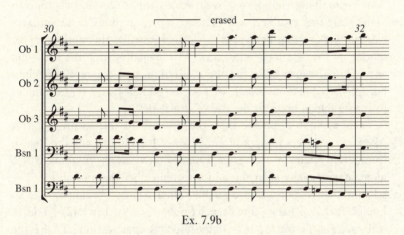

Ex. 7.9b

the monumentality of movements like *Zadok the Priest* or the Israelite's scene in *Esther* (see p. 69) is implicit in their opening bars, a skill Handel had displayed all his life. As Donald Tovey observed of *Israel in Egypt*, 'The composer who gets as far as the first twelve bars of "Sweet rose and lily" must be intending to go much farther, and shows every sign of being able to do so.'[5] In the earlier 'Concerto' versions of this material the trumpets/horns add an epilogue after bar 43, repeating the cadential bars, just as they had opened the movement, alone. Handel eliminates this individuality in *Fireworks Music*, in favour of solid homophony, suggesting that he probably did *not* want the silence before the Adagio filled with extempore solo cadenzas. Over these very bars an inscription has been firmly erased but can be partially deciphered as 'alla b . . . . de Guerre'. Might this, one wonders, have been the moment for those eighteen cannon to produce a 'bruit de guerre'? – a typical French direction, used by Rameau in *Dardanus*, Couperin in *La Steinquerque* and *La Triomphante*, and Philidor in his three *Préludes Pour le Bruit de Guerre* (in *Marches et Batteries de Tambour*, 1705).[6]

Handel gives titles to the movements representing peace and rejoicing but no title for the *battaglia*; he probably thought it too obvious. This **Allegro** is a *vin d'assemblage*, a compendium of devices, rather as the facade of Servandoni's temple contained every expected mythological reference to war and peace: fanfares, dotted cavalry rhythms, hornpipe figures (implying confidence), well-worn battle scales and rhythms, a rising-scale fugue subject and even attempted grouting of semiquaver passage-work from other sources. But there are also the motives representing peace (the long note, scale-wise melodies in 74ff.) following encouragingly soon after the 'Fire!' rhythm, and the resolution into hornpipe syncopations which are both very English and very confident (compare 'Dopo notte' at the end of *Ariodante*).

Even without a specific title, the message of the opening of this Allegro is of forces in opposition. It is not hard to imagine the British trumpets in fanfare pitted against French dotted cavalry rhythms, with a momentary *Lentement* in the minor to remember the mortalities. The scheme of alternation is unpredictably varied in length, beginning with an English fanfare (2 bars) + the French cavalry (3 bars), then E (2) + F (2), a scalar section and full *battaglia*; in the middle section we find E2 + F3, the scalar section varied, then E2 + E2 + F2, finally a rally for the cavalry with seven bars and an ensuing *battaglia*. Such dissection may seem simplistic but this was music for all, and the direct imagery of literal warfare is not inappropriate. The public had not forgotten that George actually led his own troops into battle at Dettingen, and his partiality for the 'rattles and toys' of military music is understandable.

The organisation of these sparring fragments is far from random; the tonal framework of the opening ensures that we are moved progressively from stable four-bar sections in D and A to a turmoil of different keys – G, D, A, E minor and B minor – each for a single bar (bars 69–73), yet

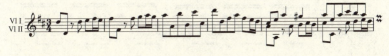

Ex. 7.10

each still within the limits of the natural brass. Then follows the 'peace motive' on a descending bass of 4, 3, 2, 1 (still surrounded by triads); after four repeats, which begin to suggest the stability of a chaconne, the direction is reversed with a rising bass 5, 6, 7, 8 back to D major (bar 94), where Handel splices in fourteen bars of his earlier material from 335a, now decorated with scales. Handel's economy shows even more in bars 99ff. (repeated at bar 162) where he lifts the harmonised version of the fugue subject *notatim* from the second movement of 335a and integrates it like one of Mattheson's *moduli*. The texture of true fugal writing would have been too thin for this 'grand plan', where single voices are never heard; here everything is doubled or delivered in triplicate, while for the indoor concerto (335a) a fugal entry was practical (Ex. 7.10).

Once again, a rising scale is the basis of this line, as it is of the long 'peace' melody in dotted minims (including the unusually high third oboe/?viola line specifically notated by Handel) in bars 78–83.

Although Handel is so openly making use of the earlier concerto movement as his catalyst, the 'grand plan' of these two movements is very different. Both have the limitations of natural brass to accommodate, but whereas in the concerto these simply play fanfares in D and A, in *Fireworks Music* they are given scalewise melodies, and appear to follow every modulation. Where the concerto is through-composed and moves quickly to the dominant (bar 27) and then through the related circle of F sharp minor and B minor before returning to D, the much longer *Fireworks Music* is sub-divided with its modulation firmly grounded in returns to D major at the close of each section; its move to B minor, the one area where the brass are not at home, is reserved for the beginning of the second section and the transitional Lentement, set dramatically apart from the remainder both in style and tempo. In part these differences are dictated by the scale: the concerto fugue runs for 107 bars, *Fireworks Music* for 140 plus a 71-bar da capo – the largest of all Handel's 'grand plans'. But he is constantly alert to small-scale, local

Ex. 7.11

improvements; even the constructionally very similar passages of semi-quavers are upgraded in *Fireworks Music* from the constant bariolage of the concerto to running patterns where Handel rings the changes in every bar even when the harmony is unvarying (compare the pedal point of bars 111–15 in *Fireworks Music* with the structurally identical bars 97–101 in the concerto shown in Ex. 7.11a and b).

In part it is the kaleidoscope of ideas that compensates for the fact that no dynamic variations are indicated in *Fireworks Music*. The suggestion in *Fiske* that 'in Green Park every instrument will have played fortis-simo' deserves some modification for *La Paix* and the smaller dances, but the effective 'crescendo-by-numbers' between bars 148 and 162 shows how Handel created alternative dynamic contouring by layering, and elsewhere by repartee. Within the potentially monotonous fanfares, Handel also avoids the literal repetitions which had marked *Water Music*

Ex. 7.12

by ingenious manipulation of the simple fanfare motive (itself related to the opening notes of the overture as well as to familiar military signals), by changing the length of phrase, taking off the last three notes and occasionally making an on-the-spot improvement of a single note; in bar 58 we can see him recharging his pen to make an alteration of a single A in the trumpet line that breaks the inevitable repetition, but still preserves formal order (Ex. 7.12). Handel's skill is in adapting a small-scale unit without sacrificing its relevance in the large-scale picture. Like the best of epic painters, he can balance the demands of the small-scale detail against the large-scale compositional whole.

From the visible alterations to the MS we can trace not only those passages where Handel considered the detail was deficient, but also those changes which were simply needed for formal strength and length. For the dominant pedal preparing the final cadence of the A section, Handel originally wrote only two bars (111–12) which led directly into 115. Finding this was too curt, and resisting the banal solution of a straight two-bar repeat, he made an attempt to simply plug the gap with material taken over literally from the earlier D major concerto, and marked for the copyist an implant of bars 13–29, some purely semiquaver passage work (the relevant indicators can be found in the earlier work). Only as a final solution did he contrive to patch in two newly composed bars of semiquavers, creating a copyist's nightmare of the end of one page and the beginning of the next, but a perfectly poised final cadence. Theatrical instinct told him the original passage was too brief, and a life-time of 'improving' persuaded him that the short cut of 'grouting' was in the end simply not good enough – inspiration plus perspiration in action. Handel's problems with the ending of this movement are indicated by the make-up of the manuscript; his first 'total' bar count of 109, as it would have been before he tinkered with bars 112–15, is written at the end of fol. 23v (bar 160) showing that at one time he considered ending the movement here. On the following page he then extends the movement by twelve bars (also indicated with an additional bar-count in the bottom right-hand corner) and writes a full cadence (bar 176). As a third stage he added a new bifolio to the manuscript on which he composed the Lentement, writing the new time-signature over the last notes of the previous page, and possibly at this late stage the idea of the da capo arose (the fermata at bar 117 is clearly a later addition).

In spite of these improvements, there are a few moments where (for the modern player at least) the notation is either ambiguous or contradictory. Note the apparent contradiction of rhythms in otherwise identical parts: between 170 and 173, for example, the horns and trumpets disagree with oboes and violins in each bar, unlike the end of the A section. There is also one technical error; Horn III has a low E in bar 62 which cannot be played without hand-stopping – a rare example of Handel in a moment of forgetfulness inattentive to the capacity of the natural horn.

The Overture essentially *is* the piece. The remaining dances are not intended to be 'introduced' by it in the manner of an opera overture or an opening chorus; they simply extend the occasion. The other movements are all shorter – bourrée and menuets by their nature, but *La Paix* and *La Réjouissance* very compact at sixteen and eighteen bars respectively. The menuets are also very regular at sixteen bars each.

To measure the distance Handel travelled in his composing life, compare the following **Bourrée** with that of WM8 (see Plate 2) and in turn with the same opening but different development of the Bourrée in *Almira*, his first opera from 1705. By 1717 he had learned to squeeze the most out of a small unit, and thus arrive at more original and less predictably 'clunky' cadences. By 1749 the peaks and troughs of the melodic line are calculated for their ensemble effect; there is even a (for Handel) surprisingly flirtatious couple of throw-away notes in bar 18 and one of the few chromatic moments in the whole suite to spice up the final eight bars; the bass-line, although in practically constant crotchet movement, spans a wider range with absolute control of the bigger picture. How far Handel has come in a composing lifetime, and yet how embedded are some of his early mannerisms, like the four-note cadential gruppetto and the repeated dactyls (but now sparing rather than obsessive) compared with his *Almira* version (see Ex. 7.13).

**La Paix** is as heavily freighted with symbolism for an eighteenth-century listener as any *battaglia*; the *alla siciliana* rhythm spells pastoral peace, coupled with birdsong (enhanced by use of flutes, to offset the

Ex. 7.13

rather unusual use of horns in avian mode), and (for us) anachronistic hints of rock-a-bye-baby. The sicilienne was not only pastoral, as used, for instance, when Bach sets the scene of the second cantata of his *Christmas Oratorio*, but was also symbolic of plenty ('He shall feed his flock'); in fact the trade, commerce and other slogans inscribed on the Machine.

The scoring and harmony underpin this message. Wide-ranging horn arpeggios (canonic as far as range will allow) avoid the obviousness of underlining the melody for the first bar and an inspired C natural in the bass line at bar 10 is used to imply the gentlest of modulations which barely takes place. Compact as the movement is, Handel seems to have had momentary doubts over how much slow music a large crowd could take; he removed the repeat mark at bar 8, but then reinstated it with a characterful 'stat' (rather than the subjunctive 'stet').

All the oboes are redeployed on two staves, to which Handel later added 'Tr et Vl' as an after-thought; these are certainly *traversi*, not

Ex. 7.14a

trumpets (although some modern editions make this mistake) since not only are the notes beyond the capacity of the natural trumpet, the very title of the movement precludes military colouring. Since extra *traverso* players would not have been standing by just for this number, we surmise that out of the total of twelve wind players given for each line, some (maybe all?) could have been oboists who doubled on flute. Alternatively, this later scoring could have been intended for the Foundling Hospital version only, since at least one flute was already required there for the Peace Anthem;[7] certainly relief for and from the oboes would be welcome by this point.

Handel's borrowings are not limited to initial themes, and there seems no justification for the theory that all he needed was a ready-made start-up idea, which he could continue by himself. Embedded in the first half of *La Paix* is a tiny contribution which may derive from Telemann's *Musique de table*, to which Handel was a subscriber.[8] But though the Quartet in question contains similar elements (the sicilienne motive, the string of trills, the drooping pairs of semiquavers, see Ex. 7.14a), a later

Ex. 7.14b

work in the same collection, the Concerto for flute, violin and strings, contains an equally strong melodic candidate, which Handel seems to have improved by the expansion of one interval (Ex. 7.14b); however, some would prefer to see it as the genuinely subconscious result of browsing through the Telemann volume, well marinaded in Handelian *gusto*, and better than either candidate.

After this movement in the MS an erased ☞ sign directs the copyist from this score to the final 'Allegro ma non troppo' of the Concerto in D (335a). There could be two explanations: since the indicator is 'lightly' erased, it could be that this movement was intended for insertion only in the Foundling Hospital concert (and would probably have concluded that version of *Fireworks Music*). Alternatively, if it was for the fireworks, then this may have been the provocation for the 'violeens' row, since the new movement depends on an alternation of winds and strings. In the event, Handel proceeded to one more symbolic movement, and two concluding menuets. Peace and Rejoicing are thus central, flanked by conventional dances that carried no class label.

The autograph clearly shows the several stages of Handel's rapid invention for **La Réjouissance**. He began with a simple symbolic fanfare movement, using only sufficient staves for trumpets and percussion, and appears to have finished the piece in this form, since the stub of the conjunct leaf (now removed) shows the remains of accolades for three four-stave systems; Handel must have removed this folio, and inserted a new bifolio on which he reworked the movement. He added 'et Hautb' to the first bar of Tr I, and their music was written onto the same staves as the trumpets. Then from bar 11 (the newly added page) Handel had room to add parts for violins and viola (had the Foundling Hospital concert just been suggested?), and finally he added an extra stave at the start (bars 1–4) for 'Violoncelli e Contra Bassi' – the barlines are clearly drawn later and not aligned with those of the staves above, showing that it was an afterthought. One loss is the canonic entry of the timpani, now obscured by the bass-line.

A Réjouissance was strictly not a dance at all, more a glorified fanfare and bustle; it can be found in many eighteenth-century suites, often but not always as a finale. Telemann offers a total of eighteen Réjouissances in his orchestral suites alone. Bach's version in Suite 4 (BWV 1069) is probably the most familiar after Handel, but contemporaries such as J. S. Endler (1694–1762) and Johann Ludwig Krebs wrote similar movements, also with three trumpets and in D major. Nor is the form exclusive to military rejoicing: 'Et resurrexit' in Bach's B minor Mass is a texted Réjouissance.

Handel in fact based his opening on two vocal numbers from an opera of nearly thirty years earlier: Giovanni Porta's *Numitore* had opened at the King's Theatre on 2 April 1720 as the first production of the new Royal Academy of Music, when Handel was Master of the Orchestra there. It had also been published by Walsh in the same year, so the two arias requisitioned must have been well known. 'Il mormorio del rio' is the starting impulse, and 'Gran nume de pastori' has a slight influence on the second half of this short movement (Ex. 7.15).

The indication 'With the Side Drum' written at the bottom of the page may refer to the (added) bass-line, or belong with the timpani, in which case the side-drums may have simply followed the rhythmic patterns suggested in the timpani line, with a roll on anything longer than a quaver. However, the original Porta aria begins with a tremolando

Ex. 7.15a

Ex. 7.15b

bass-line imitating either a continuous drum roll or the 'murmuring of the stream' (see Ex. 7.15a above), both of which hint at the possibility of the side-drums 'warbling', as Handel describes it in *Joshua*, with longer continuous rolls; his instructions leave the choice to the players.[9]

The same reasons justify the final **Menuets I and II** here as with *Water Music* and the *Concerto made from Choruses* (HWV 332): the dance was timeless, classless and unprogrammatic. In this masculine context of 'trumpets, and other martial instruments' it is important to remember that the minuet was not effete. We are told by Hans von Fleming (*Der volkommene Teutsche Soldat*, 1726) that military music was as necessary in peace as in war, to assist marching, as an accompaniment both for mourning and rejoicing, and as an aid to recruitment; moreover, the musicians serenaded their colonel in the morning and evening with 'marches, entrées and minuets'. Economy prevails for the final movements of *Fireworks Music*. The theme of Menuet I was adapted from the second movement of HWV 335b, put into the minor – Handel's mind (or desk) was obviously still full of the recent theatrical concertos. The second part follows dutifully (and symbolically?) a third below for every note of the piece. The final Menuet II had already been written as the third movement of the Overture to the *Occasional Oratorio*, where Handel decided to replace it with a more bellicose *Marche*; it already included a viola line. An earlier wind version also exists (HWV 411) dateable to *c.* 1725.

We find the same canonic downwards entries for brass as in *La Paix* bar 1. Both in the *Occasional Oratorio* and *Fireworks Music* Handel uses double-length bars, essentially writing a menuet in 6/4, as a dancer would have sensed it; in neither version is the melodic line tied between bars 14 and 15 (although it is very tempting). Handel's instructions manage to mix as many languages as possible ('La seconda volta *colli* Corni da Caccia, Hautbois et Bassons. La terza volta *tutti insieme and the Side Drums*') but apart from this variety, the movement returns to the D major simplicity of the opening of *Fireworks Music*; there is not a single accidental in this concluding dance.

The music was speedily published in parts by John Walsh (first advertised on 2 June 1749 and issued on the 25th); he included all the movements in the autograph under the title of *The Musick for the Royal Fireworks in all its Parts viz. French Horns, Trumpets, Kettle Drums, Violins, Hoboys, Violoncello, & Bassoons. with a Thorough Bass for the Harpsicord or Organ*. The second bassoon and contrabassoon were omitted entirely, and no viola part was offered, but figuring was provided for the bass-line. A later issue added the words 'Handel's Fire Musick' before the Ouverture, and there were several arrangements for 'German Flute, Violin or Harpsicord' issued over the next forty years. The first printed score appeared in Samuel Arnold's edition in 1788.

In spite of its one appearance, the ensemble assembled for the outdoor *Fireworks Music* exerted an effect on future military music. There had never been so large a wind band assembled before and would not be again until Berlioz's *Symphonie Funèbre et Triomphale* (1840). A wind band, which today implies amateurs before professionals (marching band, brass band, etc.) was in the eighteenth century a strictly professional entity. Soon after the peace celebrations these musicians were developed into an ensemble capable of more than just signalling; in 1762 the Royal Artillery raised a 'Band of Musick' including clarinets, one of the predeccesors of the modern military band, and, in a curious reversal of the days of *Water Music*, the band of the Coldstream Guards resigned en masse in the same year when asked to accompany an 'aquatic excursion'; however, their places were taken by musicians recruited from Hanover.

The *Musick for the Royal Fireworks* was only once performed as first planned – and even then a pyrotechnical hitch deflected the public interest. Maybe it was the most expensive background music ever for the royal tour of the Machine, and quite possibly less audible to the large Georgian crowd than the number of players would suggest or Handel might have hoped. Its original setting has never since been recreated, although firework displays of quite different design often call on recorded Handel for accompaniment, usually insisting that the pyro-technics be coordinated with the music, to the detriment of both. No doubt the combination of patriotic and commercial sentiment would be unpalatable today, though it is surprising that Victorian England did not embrace it for Crystal Palace spectaculars. In fact, neither *Water Music* nor *Fireworks Music* seem to have found a place in nineteenth-century concert-giving, which preferred choral affirmation, and it was left to the twentieth century to revive and record these 'splendid freaks', some-times in the oddest of transformations.

# 8

## Handel in other hands

On no account whatever would I interpolate marks of expression, *tempi*, &c., or anything else, in a score of Handel's, if there is to be any doubt whether they are mine or his; and as he has marked his *pianos* and *fortes*, and figured bass wherever he thought them essential, I must either leave these out altogether, or place the public under the impossibility of discovering which are his marks, and which are mine ... I am sure you are not angry with me for stating my opinion so candidly? it is too closely connected with all that I have considered right, during the whole course of my life, for me now to give it up.

(Mendelssohn to Moscheles, 7 March 1845, on editing *Israel in Egypt*)[1]

Within a few years of the royal excursion some numbers from *Water Music* were absorbed into the canon of popular, almost ballad repertoire (with bass-lines that were not Handel's). Two minuets were used by John Gay and Pepusch in *Polly*, the sequel to *The Beggar's Opera*, in 1729: the Horn Minuet (WM7) in C, curiously called 'Trumpet Minuet' with the words 'Abroad after misses most husbands will roam', and the real Trumpet Minuet (WM22) as a rousing 'Cheer up my lads' (in G).

Other vocal refits produced 'Hark how the Trumpet Sounds (The Soldiers call to the War) Set to the French horn Minuet' (*c.*1720) and 'Cloe when I view thee Smiling. Words to a celebrated Minuet of Mr. Handell's' (*c.*1725), while the Trumpet Minuet served for both 'Phillis the Lovely. A Song the words by M^r Kirkland' and 'Thyrsis, afflicted with Love and Despair. A Song to M^r Hendel's Trumpet Minuet'. The Horn and Trumpet Minuets outstripped all other movements in popular circulation, and were actually the first items of *Water Music* to appear in print, as two keyboard lessons 'by Mr Hendell' in 1720 (see p. 24). Extra movements published by Daniel Wright *c.*1733 as *The Famous Water Peice Compos'd by Mr. Handel* included a version of WM11 in D for

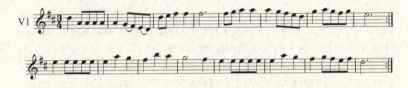

Ex. 8.1

single trumpet, and a transposition of the *Marche* found in *Partenope* (17) in B flat. The three other movements (Allegro, Aire and another March) are so far unidentified, but our old friend John Grano published a version of the *Partenope* march under his own name as 'The Lord Mayor's March' (*Musica Bellicosa*, Walsh, 1730) so he may have had a hand in this collection. This is piratical territory; Wright was described by John Hawkins as 'a man who never printed anything he did not steal'. On the other hand very little from *Fireworks Music* was repeated after its initial year. Walsh offered it 'set for the German flute, violin or harpsicord' in 1749, but the Harrison print of *c.* 1795 'for the voice, harpsichord, and violin' is a misprint; sadly, there are no vocal pyrotechnics.

All eighteenth-century arrangements of both pieces were reductions and simplifications. The intriguing four part 'Oxford' version of *Water Music* has already been mentioned (p. 47), but stranger transformations overtook the most popular pieces: WM22, the Trumpet Minuet, retitled Menuetto, is transposed to A in a version for bass viol[2] seemingly derived from the HWV 546 version in *A General Collection of Minuets* (London, 1729). The appropriate trills and slurs which are missing in the full version are added to bars 4 and 6 but the bass-line, as ever, is rewritten and the reiterated quavers which are such a feature of the cadential bars are reduced to crotchets in bars 15 and 23. In the third volume of *The Dancing Master*, Playford's perennially popular collection, reissued *c.* 1727, the Horn Minuet, transposed to D, comes with the instruction: 'This Dance must be done with the Minuet step; and each Straine play'd twice.'[3] Here the cadences are also adapted and a couple of useful slurs added (Ex. 8.1).

All these alternatives are relevant today, as the snobbism attached to 'original' versions begins to accept 'contemporary arrangements' with more enthusiasm. Some of the minuet songs can still be surprisingly effective, especially if reunited with the composer's bass-line; it is odd that while the equivalent adaptations from Purcell's output appear regularly in recital, the same exposure is not extended to Handel. Keyboard players could also reconsider the transcriptions which in the eighteenth century were the most popular of all Handel's keyboard works.

Serious damage was done during Handel's lifetime by the editions of John Walsh, and many garbled texts remained to be untangled by the Arnold and Chrysander editions. Arnold's impressive (but unfinished) project sent ripples through the musical world; Beethoven subscribed to it, and advised Archduke Rudolf, his pupil and also patron, 'not to forget Handel's works, as they always offer the best nourishment for your ripe musical mind, and will at the same time lead to admiration for this great man'. The publications of the German Handel Society, largely the achievement of Friedrich Chrysander (1858–1902, with the last volumes being issued after his death) were for a long time the only coherent complete source, now being replaced by the HHA, started in 1955 and still in progress.

In terms of performances rather than editions of these works, there is less to discuss before the twentieth century. The 1784 Handel Commemoration in London did not offer *Water Music* or *Fireworks Music*, but nevertheless still observed the proportions of the Handelian orchestra, albeit multiplied by a large factor (forty-eight first violins balanced by thirteen first oboes still follows the three- or four-to-one ratio). The 1859 Crystal Palace commemoration differed enormously, of course, with a huge chorus and large string body but few woodwinds. But the nineteenth century was more critical of tampering with earlier texts in print than we sometimes assume. When Mozart's arrangement of *Messiah* (with further additions by Johann Hiller) was performed at Covent Garden in 1805, the response from the *Sun* was:

> We entertain a very high respect for the genius of Mozart, but we also hold the unrivalled powers of Handel in due reverence, and therefore must enter our protest against any such alterations in works that have obtained the sanction of time and of the best musical judges.

It was the enthusiasm of the ever-larger choral societies of the nineteenth century that kept many of Handel's oratorios alive, while the operas and much of his instrumental music was relegated to 'student' and 'extract' usage or else completely ignored.

Credit for the return of both *Water Music* and *Fireworks Music* to the concert hall rests with Hamilton Harty, who re-orchestrated six movements from *Water Music* for the Hallé Orchestra, and conducted them in Manchester in 1920.[4] The sequence of Allegro, Air, Bourrée, Hornpipe, Andante espressivo, Allegro deciso (alla Hornpipe) (i.e. WM 3, 6, 8, 9, 4, 12) begins in F and ends in D, using WM4 to bridge the gap, rather as Handel used WM10. Within this scheme, however, Harty mixed portions of other movements, such as adding the F minor section of WM 7 to the Air (and creating a Mahlerian postlude by repeating the first phrase of the Air deliciously scored with four muted horns). His wind section also included flutes and clarinets, but, following Handel, he saved the trumpets for the D major finale.

Following up the success of the *Suite from the Water Music* with a similar treatment of *Fireworks Music* in 1923, Harty imposed more restraint on the orchestra (no flutes or clarinets) and used rather more of the original movements, but shortened and reorganised; the Overture lost its Lentement and da capo, *La Paix* followed with the *Bourrée* after it, and the first minuet became a trio to the second. This suite did not repeat the success of his *Water Music* transcription, which was issued as an acoustic recording in 1922 (although we are told that 'attempts at recording began on 13 December 1920').[5]

If Harty's experiments aimed at 'a richer and fuller harmonic dress, but without altering the basic structure' (as his programme notes claimed), the rival suite produced by Leopold Stokowski five years later was unrestrained, indeed full-frontal sonic competition. He took the same movements as Harty had chosen, but orchestrated them with rather more abandon, and also issued the result on record in 1934. Twenty-five years later he returned to the suite and added two new movements, curiously beginning with WM2, thus starting the suite on a first-inversion dominant harmony. The solo oboe (originally Robert Bloom) gets 'stylistically authentic baroque ornaments . . . written out in the Maestro's manuscript'.[6] The Air is interrupted by the opening statement of WM7 on solo horns, and then returns *pianissimo*, and a snare-drum is added in the Hornpipe together with piccolo and the taped sounds of 'fireworks and children cavorting' at the end.

A surprisingly early inclination towards 'historical principles' is encountered with the war-time film 'The Great Mr Handel', made in 1942 as the
first production of J. Arthur Rank; ever a good Methodist, he chose a subject
combining religion and music. Ernest Irving, the music director, was a
declared Handelian; he had already used parts of *Water Music* in another
patriotic venture, 'Find, Fix and Strike' (1942), and the budget allowed for
this drama of 'Handel ruined but rising again' gave him wider scope:

> Nearly all the music is Handel's. With so much of Tweedledum, there
> must be a little of Tweedledee, and so I have inserted a little tune of
> Buononcini, and there are some traditional street cries of the period. One
> of these is based on a motet by Orlando Gibbons. But with these small
> exceptions, the music is entirely Handel's.
>
> Some of the score is precisely as Handel wrote it. For instance, in the
> Fireworks music (played in Vauxhall Gardens) I have removed the
> extraneous timpani and trombone parts thus bringing to light Handel's
> cunning device of using the violas as a sort of bass trumpet, a tromba
> marina, in fact. Not a note has been altered or added to Handel, but in the
> orchestration I have given to the wind instruments chords or progressions
> which may well have formed part of Handel's improvisation on his own
> figure-bass [*sic*].
>
> In the scoring I have not used clarinets as Handel seldom employed
> them. The London Philharmonic Orchestra, who recorded the music
> under my direction, were kind enough to remove all the metal junk with
> which modern orchestral string-instruments are bedizened and to sub-
> stitute gut, as used in the days of our forefathers.
>
> It was a great task to find gut strings for this adventure, but we were able
> to run to earth a little hoard in a fiddle-maker's shop. The difference in tone
> is, to my mind, like that between silk and fustian. I borrowed two Kirkman
> harpsichords, one from Morley, the harp maker, and the other from the
> Chaplin sisters, famous for their association with the 'Beggar's Opera' . . .
>
> A good deal of the action takes place about 1738, when Handel was
> rehearsing Serse (Xerxes) at Covent Garden,[7] and several quotations are
> made from its score . . . Part of the Water music and other famous best-
> sellers of the great master are heard either in the foreground or the
> background . . .
>
> . . . I have had the advantage of working from a copy of the earliest
> published score [of Messiah], bought by subscription for the Wakefield
> Club in 1766. I have taken the liberty to disregard some remarks made in
> the preface to his edition by Ebenezer Prout, with which, in all respects,

I disagree. I think, for instance, that if Handel wanted a demi-semi-quaver he knew how to write one, and that the clash of rhythms in 'Surely He hath borne our griefs' was intentional, and directed to a particular effect.

The whole work of arranging the music was congenial and refreshing. What a grand fellow Handel was, even apart from his music ... generous and kind of heart, and an indomitable fighter. This age could do with men of high character and undeviating integrity of thinking and living, like George Frederic Handel.[8]

The remaining reception history in the twentieth century, much of it preserved on recordings, follows two channels. One has been the splitting of *Water Music* into three suites, a scheme first put into practice by Thurston Dart in the 1950s,[9] based on a performing edition of the complete *Water Music* made by Brian Priestman, relying primarily on *Lennard* and *Walsh*. Dart proposed the F major suite for the up-river trip, the G major suite indoors and D major for the return, but this is firmly contradicted by Bonet (and by the length of time for the journey in both directions). Regrettably, this division has been reinforced in *Redlich*, by Bernd Baselt in the numbering of the HWV catalogue and countless performances since.

The other development has been the emergence of a performance protocol that follows the purist ideals espoused by Mendelssohn in editing – that the composer and his expectations are innocent until proved guilty. This trend was marked first by a return to Handel's original scoring. The complete indoor *Fireworks Music* was recorded by the Berlin Philharmonic under Fritz Lehmann on 9–10 November 1952,[10] and was later adopted by chamber orchestras (Hans von Benda and the Berlin Chamber Orchestra recorded the later F major versions of WM11 and 12 on 78s in 1948, and followed this with selections from *Fireworks Music*). Charles Mackerras made the first recording with modern instruments of the all-wind version of *Fireworks Music* on the 200th anniversary of Handel's death (14 April 1959). A recording time of midnight was dictated by the pressures of London's musical life, since only then could the necessary number of wind and brass players be free. Like Stokowski, he also added sound-effects of fireworks but on a separate repeat of the final Minuet on the disc.[11] The published score, very fully marked up in 'period' style, was edited by Mackerras and Anthony Baines (Oxford University Press, 1960).

Later came the appearance of ensembles of historically appropriate instruments, starting with August Wenzinger's all-wind *Fireworks Music* with the 'Bläservereinigung der Archiv Produktion' plus two *Concerti a due cori* (HWV 333 and 334) with the Konzertgruppe der Schola Cantorum Basiliensis in 1962, and *Water Music* (reorganised into three suites and with a continuo section containing two lutes, harp and harpsichord), recorded in September 1965.[12]

To balance the 'period' tendency, we are well supplied with examples of other 'refurbishments': a transcription of *Fireworks Music* for piano sextet by S. Robjohns was published in 1927 and the D major *Water Music* Hornpipe was arranged for four pianos and recorded by 'The First Piano Quartet' *c*. 1950.[13] More recently we have a range of styles from the vocal gymnastics of The Swingles and the Moog synthesizer of Wendy (Walter) Carlos to the arrangements (of *Water Music* and *Fireworks Music*) by Keigo Tsunoda for the virtuoso New Koto Ensemble of Tokyo, a recent jazz gloss by Jacques Loussier and some confrontational electronic offerings on <MP3.com>. Luckily, this music is vandal-proof.

Of earlier adaptations, neither the vocal or keyboard arrangements of the eighteenth century have made any come-back as yet, nor the useful adaptations for two horns or two trumpets from Grano and his colleagues. Nor are there yet any performances or recordings which combine some of the pre-existing material which Handel appropriated alongside the results of his borrowings, nor a *Fireworks Music* as it might have been presented at the Foundling Hospital.

In all important decisions, each of the recorded versions mentioned above comes to a different conclusion – edition, sequence, size of ensemble, types of instruments, tempi, decorations and so on. To help listeners distinguish amongst the variety of past performances, and to assist performers involved in present or future renditions, a summary of these parameters follows.

# 9

## *Performance parameters*

> The great thing is to make sure that we like the style we chose better than
> we like any other, that we engraft on it whatever we hear that we think will
> be a good addition, and depart from it wherever we dislike it.
>
> (Samuel Butler on 'Anachronism')[1]

Questions of performance practice are today as relevant to the interested
and critical listener as to the 'Historically Informed Performer'. Many
specific suggestions deriving from compositional evidence have been
discussed in the preceding text, but extra 'HIP' points never mentioned
or taken for granted by Handel also need to be addressed since they affect
not only what the performer plays but what the listener chooses to hear.

### Which suites?

A first option for playing the whole *Water Music* set should be to preserve
the original sequence. If extracting separate suites, try to achieve a suitable
shape, with both a start and a finish. For the 'Horn Suite', adding Handel's
revised horn numbers, 11 and 12, or using the adapted sequence of the
*Aylesford* score and parts is a help. The 'Trumpet Suite' is musically
balanced, providing the trumpeters are not resistant to playing five consecutive movements without a break. The 'Flute Suite' should either be
avoided as an entity or else filled out with movements from outside *Water
Music*. Consider using the 'Oxford' version, or a sequence derived from it.

The choice of wind or strings for *Fireworks Music* is determined by
whether the performance is indoor or outdoor; try ending an indoor
*Fireworks Music* with 'Allegro ma non troppo' of the Concerto in D,
HWV 335a, as a finale after *La Paix* (with or without an 'ad libitum'
movement before it). If fireworks are included in the outdoor version,
they *follow* the music.

## How many instruments?

In his orchestral ensembles Handel preserved a ratio of roughly one oboe for every three or four violins; thus the wind ensemble of both *Water Music* and *Fireworks Music* (in its indoor version) should have at least four oboes, and between two and four bassoons. 'Flauti piccoli' are also specified in the plural, which leaves only the *traverso* and the brass players in *Water Music* as one to a part. There is only one 'oboe solo' in the whole of *Water Music* and *Fireworks Music*, but the *Concerti a due cori* certainly specify oboe solos, even if more players per part are used for the tuttis, with possibly two bassoons on each bass-line. Replacing some or all of the oboes with flutes in *La Paix* is probably beyond the capacity of any but a contract orchestra.

Research is still required into the possible evidence of eighteenth-century seating (or even standing) plans. Some differences between opera and oratorio disposition can be deduced from engravings, but the question of how to draw a third violin part from Violins I and II remains unanswered, especially if the two sections are antiphonal.

## Interpreting the notation

After a period of popularity, the modern enthusiasm for 'reconciling' Handel's notation has flagged and opinion leans to the view that he may actually have meant what he wrote. Conventions of the *alla francese* style, tirades and 'double dotting' (as Arnold Dolmetsch christened it) may not require on-the-page adaptation. Thus, given a suitable tempo, upbeats may mix both quavers and semiquavers, and again (tempo permitting) tirades can be played by violins with separate bows, not one long slur. Simultaneous triplets and dotted rhythms will usually be assimilated, but it is worth debating whether the slurs in WM16 imply a bowing, or are simply the contemporary notation for triplets. The rhythmic implications of Muffat's suggested bowing in WM16 have been discussed on p. 42.

A flexibility of *notation*, rather than *interpretation*, is implied by the rhythmic differences in FM1, or a comparison of the keyboard version of WM6 with the full score – the eighteenth-century composer transmitted intention rather than instruction. By all means contrast, for example, the various transformations of the *Fireworks Music* opening; there are several rhythmic variants which might or might not lend their weight to theories on rhythmic alteration in performance. One would think that the version written for the largest numbers and the least rehearsal time would display the least ambiguous notation, but this is not the case.

## Instruments

The most corrigible string part (in modern editions) is the viola line, sometimes garbled in *Water Music* and an after-thought in *Fireworks Music*. Handel's 'col bassi' or 'col Tromba III' are only partially useful as instructions for extrapolating a viola line, which may sometimes be in unison and sometimes at the octave according to eighteenth-century practice. The solution proposed by *Chrysander* and earlier editions, for instance, in the first half of *La Réjouissance* is very unlikely, almost all on the bottom string and crossing below the bass-line in bar 8. See *Fiske* for the best solution to date.

Brass parts are traditionally the least marked lines in all eighteenth-century scores, and much of the finesse in delivery was probably taught only within the guilds. Handel's indication of 'Bebung' for horns in the alternative WM11 (see Ex. 3.9) is an exception to the rule, as are his dynamic markings in WM5. Evidence of contemporary military performance would suggest that slurs were added to the trumpet fanfares starting in bar 47 of *Fireworks Music*. The impossible and wrong notes in the horn writing have been discussed on pp. 31, 33 and 112. Handel marks only one roll for the timpani in bar 42 of FM1 (and none in the earlier version). It is worth considering that players should refrain from any *ad libitum* behaviour before immediately succumbing to the easy excitement of a rousing roll in bar 37 of that movement. The more varied options for side-drums 'warbling' (since their parts are not notated) have already been discussed (pp. 116–17) along with a plea for multiple side-drums if possible.

## Continuo

A continuo instrument is not essential to either piece and is certainly wasted in the open air. Figures were added to the bass-line for publication, but almost certainly not by Handel, who took care that there should be no harmonic gaps if a chordal instrument is absent (see, for example, the viola part in WM18). Indoor performances may have included harpsichord, lute or harp, but an organ only when it formed part of an oratorio. Thurston Dart suggested that the very scant figuring in two movements of *Water Music* in the *Lennard* MS (see p. 22) meant that these alone were the movements where he considered continuo indispensable, though there is no evidence to support this; if Handel wanted to silence the continuo as a special effect, he would normally indicate *senza cembalo*. The figuring published by Walsh is very fallible (it is not included in *Fiske*) and needs a thorough overhaul if it is to be used today.

## Repeats

The question of applying a da capo formula to pairs of dances remains open; a few are suggested in some sources, though in general the early eighteenth century did not treat a second minuet as a trio. The instructions for repeats 'trois fois' are explicit but for concert purposes sometimes too lengthy; a solution can be to alternate wind and brass scoring for each section, and add a da capo without repeats for the full ensemble (i.e. $A^1$, $A^2$, $B^1$, $B^2$, $A^3$, $B^3$).

## Tempi

Handel's erasures, rarely reported in modern editions, surely imply a meaningful change of mind, often as regards tempo; when he specially altered 'Menuet' to 'Minuet' and deleted 'Allegro' for the last movement of HWV 332 we must suspect some significance. The erased 'Largo' at the opening of *Fireworks Music* can suggest (despite the markings on earlier versions of this material) that Handel felt a less funereal tempo would be more appropriate here. When in doubt, it is good to remember his 'Allegro così così' (in Op. 7 no. 4) and other favourite markings such as 'Andante allegro' and 'Tempo ordinario'.

## Ornamentation

There is little opportunity for added embellishment (other than conventional cadential trills, etc.) since there is only one appropriate solo

(WM2). The notated decorations of Giuseppe Sammartini make his oboe works a suitable reference point for ornamental style after the late 1720s when he became Handel's soloist at the King's Theatre[2] and the *XII Solos ... with proper Graces adapted to each Adagio* which William Babell published in 1725 are another potential quarry. Other additions to Handel's notation (such as the slurred semiquaver pairs sometimes adopted in *La Paix*) need not be numerous. Revealing though Handel's borrowings are of his compositional methods, they rarely help with specific performance questions; the transformations that produced the Lentement of *Water Music* or the opening of *Fireworks Music* demonstrate as much, and such evidence belongs in the kitchen, not on the dining table.

A final suggestion, not intended to shoot our title topic in the foot, would be an encouragement, when either of these suites is feeling a little over-exposed, even *dépassé*, or when the requisite forces and colours are not available (no recorders, for instance, for *Water Music*, no side-drums for *Fireworks Music*), to widen the focus on Handel's entertainment music and offer an alternative selection of his genius. Since he would have never presented the same material in public quite so many times without alteration, one could suggest making an 'alternative Water Music' from similar material found throughout his stage works (as for instance Thomas Beecham did – though forgoing the cosmetic orchestrations he wished on these pieces).[3] The novelty of a suite drawn from *Almira, Ariodante, Il Pastor Fido, Rodrigo, Terpsichore* and many similar and available sources would signal a welcome reinvestment in Handel's lifelong principles of independence, enterprise and variety.

# Appendix
## Sources of shared material

### Water Music

**WM 1**    For the fugue subject (first eight notes), see keyboard fugue in E major *c*. 1717–20 (HWV 612).

**WM 3**    Compare bars 7–11 with *Amadigi*, 'Desterò dall'empia dite', bars 29–33.

**WM 4**    Compare Handel Op.1/6 mvt 1, Andante larghetto (HWV 364a).

**WM 5**    Possibly related to Keiser, *Octavia*, aria 'Streu' Blumen aus Idumen', bars 1–4 (cf. WM, bars 8–10).

**WM 6**    Antiphon 'Haec est Regina virginum', (HWV 235) bar 1 (cf. WM, bars 1–2).

**WM 11**    Keiser, *La forza della virtù*, aria 'Hör auf, mein Herz, zu sagen' (or 'Mein Hertz, hör auf zu sagen'), cf. bars 1–5 and 29–30. Also used for Concerto in F HWV 331 bars 1–5.

**WM 12**    Opening used in *Amadigi*, 'Sento la gioia, ch'in sen mi brilla'; also later in Handel Sonata Op. 1/9, mvt 2 for middle section (HWV 367b). See also Cantata 'Stanco di più soffrire', aria 'Se più non t'amo,' HWV 167 (1708), also found in Cantata 'Dolce pur', HWV 109, cf. WM, bars 5–7 and 62–3. There is another unrelated borrowing from *Teseo*, 'È pur bello', bars 4–7 (cf. WM, bars 24–7).

**WM 16**    Keiser, *Claudius*, chorus 'ô Evan Evoë' Act 3, scene 8, bars 1–10 (=WM bars 1–2, 5–6). Also used in *Pastor Fido* Act I ballet music for 'Danse Pour les Chasseurs'.

**WM 17**    *La Resurrezione*, chorus 'Il nume vincitor', bars 1–4 (cf. WM, bars 1–4).

**WM 22**    Keiser, *Der Carneval von Venedig (Der angenehme Betrug, oder Der Carneval von Venedig)* 1707, 'Aria en Menuet' for Celinde, 'Ach Liebe bilde dir dieses nicht ein'.

## Music for the Royal Fireworks

| | |
|---|---|
| **Ouverture** | Johann Philipp Krieger, *Aria* [and 24 variations] for keyboard. |
| **La Paix** | Telemann, *Musique de table I*, 1733, Quartet, mvt 1, bars 1–6 and/or *Musique de table I*, Konzert, mvt 3, bars 1–6. |
| **Réjouissance** | Giovanni Porta, *Numitore* (1720), aria 'Il mormorio del rio', also aria 'Gran nume de pastori'. Also very similar to Rameau's 'Entr'acte en place d'une Ouverture', in *Naïs* Act 1 (1749). |
| **Menuet 1** | Theme adapted from HWV 335b mvt 2, put into the minor. |
| **Menuet 2** | Taken from *Occasional Oratorio*; see also HWV 422 for 2 oboes, 2 horns and BC in G major (1746/7) which is followed by another Menuet. The second part may be based on that of the minuet in the overture to Bononcini's *Xerse*. |

## Concerto HWV 332

| | |
|---|---|
| **1. Ouverture** | Later adapted for *Alexander Balus* transposed to D major. |
| **2. Allegro ma non troppo** | *Messiah* (1741), 'And the Glory of the Lord' (bars 73–87 cut). |
| **3. Allegro** | *Belshazzar* (1744), 'See from his post Euphrates flies'. |
| **4. Largo** | *Ottone* (1722), 'S'io dir potessi'. |
| **5. A tempo ordinario** | *Semele* (1743), 'Lucky omens bless our rites'. |
| **6. Alla breve moderato** | *Semele*, 'Attend the pair'. |
| **7. Minuet** | *Lotario* (1729), 'Non t'inganni la speranza' and *Alexander Balus*, 'Thrice happy the monarch' (1747). |

## Concerto HWV 333

| | |
|---|---|
| **1. Pomposo** | *Esther* (first version, 1720), 'Jehova crown'd'. |
| **2. Allegro** | *Esther* (first version), 'He comes to end our woes'. |
| **3. A tempo giusto** | *Messiah* (1741), 'Lift up your heads'. |
| **4. Largo** | *Esther* (first version), 'Ye sons of Israel, mourn'. |
| **5. Allegro ma non troppo** | *Esther* (second version, 1732), 'Thro' the nations he shall be next in dignity' (also 'Let rolling streams their gladness show' from *Ode for the Birthday of Queen Anne*). |

| | |
|---|---|
| **6. A tempo ordinario** | *Occasional Oratorio*, 'God found them guilty'. |

## Concerto HWV 334

| | |
|---|---|
| **1. Ouverture** | Overture in D for 2 clarinets and horn (HWV 424). |
| **5. Andante larghetto** | Keiser, *Octavia*, 'Wallet nicht zu laut'. Also *Partenope* 15; Telemann, *Harmonischer Gottesdienst* III, Cantata 34/2; *Belshazzar*, air 'The leafy honours'. See also *Judas Maccabeus*, air 'So rapid thy course is', bars 5–6 (cf. WM, bars 45–6). |
| **6. Allegro** | Material from *Partenope*, aria Rosmira 'Io seguo sol fiero tra boschi le belve' (Finale of Act I); also from Telemann, *Harmonischer Gottesdienst*, Cantata 34/2 (a source Handel had used frequently in *Solomon*). |

## Overture in D for 2 clarinets and horn (HWV 424)

| | |
|---|---|
| **1. Ouverture** | Shared with HWV 334, mvt 1. |
| **4. Andante allegro** | Giovanni Porta, *Numitore*, aria 'Sol m'affanna' bars 1–6. |

# Notes

## The character of the man

1 See Jacob Simon (ed.), *Handel: A Celebration of his Life and Times* (London, 1985), pp. 40–2. There are many versions of the caricature, the gouache version in the Fitzwilliam Museum, Cambridge, probably being the picture listed in the artist's sale of 23 March 1765: 'An Hog playing on an Organ, with various embellishments, all Emblematical'. This has an alternative set of 'emblems' including an owl perched on Handel's head ('deceit' or 'wisdom'?) and on a scroll the words 'Pension Benefit Nobility Friendship' alongside 'Pax'. See also Richard W. Wallace, 'Joseph Goupy's Satire on George Frideric Handel' in *Apollo* 117 (February 1983), 104–5. 'I am myself alone' is Gloucester after murdering Henry in *The Third Part of Henry VI*, Act 5, scene 6.

2 J. S. Bach, letter of 28 October 1730.

3 'Commonplace Book', James Osborne Collection, Beinecke Rare Book and Manuscript Library, Yale University, 428–33: 'Was ein virtuose, so in London kommt, zu observiren sol'; translation by Harold E. Samuel from *The Musical Times*, September 1981, p. 591.

4 Lord Hervey, *Memoirs of the Reign of George the Second* (London, 1848), p. 273.

5 Simon, *Handel*, p. 175.

6 See Peggy Ellen Daub, 'Music at the Court of George II' (Ph.D. thesis, Cornell University, 1985).

7 See Christopher Hailey's review, *JAMS* 56 (2) (2003), 484ff., from which the following quotations are taken.

8 Translation from David Charlton and Sarah Hibberd, 'My father was a poor Parisian musician' ['Mémoires d'un musicien'], *Journal of the Royal Musical Association* 128 (2) (2003).

## Politics and power

1 Donald Burrows, 'Handel and Hanover', in Peter Williams (ed.), *Bach, Handel, Scarlatti: Tercentenary Essays* (Cambridge, 1985), pp. 35ff.

2 John Mainwaring, *Memoirs of the Life of the Late George Frederic Handel* (London, 1760), p. 72.

3 Six excursions in the summer of 1715 alone are documented; Donald Burrows and Robert D. Hume, 'George I, the Haymarket Opera Company and Handel's *Water Music*', *Early Music* 19 (3) (1991), 323–41.

4 *Ibid.*, 333, with the added proviso that 'he was either a genuine lover of opera or a masochist'.

5 Mainwaring, *Memoirs*, pp. 91–2.

6 See more details in Howard Serwer, 'The World of the *Water Music*', *Händel-Jahrbuch* 1996/7, pp. 101–11.

7 Burrows and Hume, 'George I', p. 333.

8 Alfred Plummer, *The London Weavers' Company, 1600–1970* (London, 1972), pp. 229–32.

9 This description formed an appendage to a letter dealing with a request from the Prussian King to buy him six negroes.

10 The double date shows the Old Style Calendar, as used in Britain, and the New Style (Gregorian) which had been adopted in the German and Netherland Protestant States since 1700.

11 Geheimes Staatsarchiv Preußischer Kulturbesitz: Rep 81 London: *Konzepte aller Relationen Bonnets, Abschriften der Eingaben an die Englische Regierung und deren Antworten, Abschriften einzelner Reskripte und anderen politischen Schreiben nebst Zeitungen und anderen Beilagen*, Nr. 12: (1716) 1717, Nr. 13: (1717) 1718; translation based on that by William Barclay Squire, *The Musical Times*, December 1922, p. 866.

12 See Donald Burrows (ed.), *The Cambridge Companion to Handel* (Cambridge, 1997), pp. 240ff.

13 *Das neu-eröffnete Orchestre* (Hamburg, 1713), p. 267.

14 [John Grano,] *Handel's Trumpeter: The Diary of John Grano*, ed. John Ginger (New York, 1998), p. 314.

15 *Ibid.*, p. 29.

16 *Ibid.*, pp. 262–4.

17 Information kindly provided by Crispian Steele-Perkins.

### Water Music

1 Definition from Roland Barthes, *A Lover's Discourse* (New York, 1978), p. 34.

2 See introduction to Donald Burrows and Martha Ronish, *A Catalogue of Handel's Musical Autographs* (Oxford, 1994) and John Roberts, 'A New Handel Aria, or Hamburg Revisited', in Klaus Hortschansky and Konstanze Musketa (eds.), *Gedenkschrift für Bernd Baselt* (Halle, 1995), p. 113.

3  See Jens Peter Larsen, *Handel's Messiah: Origins, Composition, Sources* (London, 1957).

4  As argued by Anthony Hicks in his sleeve-notes to the recording made in 1983 by the English Concert (DGG Archiv 4717232).

5  William C. Smith, *Concerning Handel, His Life and Works: Essays* (London, 1948), p. 271.

6  See above, n. 3.

7  For more information on the variety of Handel's dance music and a thematic listing see Sarah McCleave, 'Handel's Unpublished Dance Music: A Perspective on his Approach to Composition', *Göttinger Händel-Beiträge* 6 (1996), 127–42.

8  For analytical descriptions of the minuet and other dance forms see Johann Mattheson's *Kern melodischer Wissenschafft* (Hamburg, 1737), pp. 110ff., which includes a mention of Handel. Also Tilden A. Russell, 'The Unconventional Dance Minuet: Choreographies of the Menuet d'Exaudet', *Acta Musicologica* 64 (1992), 124n for the absence of trios in early eighteenth-century dance tutors, and more information on danced minuets.

9  See Franklin B. Zimmerman, 'Musical Borrowings in the English Baroque', *Musical Quarterly* 52 (4) (1966), 493–5, disproving Winton Dean's assertion that this overture is 'one of the few without borrowing'.

10  It would seem that the piece was originally scored for a single oboe.

11  Sibley Music Library, Rochester, NY: shelf-mark Vault M2. 1 D172. See Tim Crawford, 'Lord Danby's Lute Book: A New Source of Handel's Hamburg Music', *Göttinger Händel-Beiträge* 2 (1986), 19–50.

12  See Donald Burrows, 'The Christ Church *Water Music* Chamber Suite: Is it an Authentic Handelian Arrangement?', *Händel-Jahrbuch* 1993, pp. 24–41 and *Water Music: Chamber Suite* (ed. Burrows) (Novello, 1991).

## The 'indebtedness' of Handel

1  *Critica Musica* (Hamburg, 1722), translation from John T. Winemiller, 'Handel's Borrowing and Swift's Bee: Handel's "Curious" Practice and the Theory of Transformative Imitation' (Ph.D. thesis, University of Chicago, 1994), p. 42.

2  Antoine François Prévost d'Exiles, *Le pour et le contre* I, 9 (Paris, 1733), pp. 207–8.

3  Johann Adolf Scheibe, *Ueber die musikalische Composition*, vol. I, *Die Theorie der Melodie und Harmonie* (Leipzig, 1773), p. 53, translation from John Roberts, 'Handel's Borrowings from Keiser', *Göttinger Händel-Beiträge* 2 (1986), 51.

4 17 January 1743; Foundling Museum, Gerald Coke Handel Collection, *Jennens/Holdsworth Letters* 2.

5 *An Account of the Musical Performances in Westminster Abbey and the Pantheon ... In Commemoration of Handel* (London, 1785), p. 39.

6 Letter of 4 March 1805, printed in Appendix I of Charles Burney, *A General History of Music*, ed. Frank Mercer (London, 1935), vol. II, p. 1038.

7 E. P. Thompson, *The Making of the English Working Class* (London, 1963).

8 John Roberts, 'Why Did Handel Borrow?' in Stanley Sadie and Anthony Hicks (eds.), *Handel Tercentenary Collection* (London, 1987).

9 Ellwood Derr, 'Handel's Procedures for Composing with Materials from Telemann's "Harmonischer Gottes-Dienst"', *Göttinger Händel-Beiträge* 1 (1984), 126–48, and John Roberts, 'Handel's Borrowings from Telemann: An Inventory', *ibid.*, 151.

10 See George J. Buelow, 'Handel's Borrowing Techniques: Some Fundamental Questions Derived from a Study of "Agrippina" (Venice, 1709)', *Göttinger Händel-Beiträge* 2 (1986), 108.

11 Johann Mattheson, *Grundlage einer Ehren-Pforte* (Hamburg, 1740), pp. 93–4.

12 See David Ross Hurley, *Handel's Muse: Patterns of Creation in his Oratorios and Musical Dramas, 1743–1751* (Oxford, 2001); also 'Handel's Compositional Process' in Donald Burrows (ed.), *The Cambridge Companion to Handel* (Cambridge, 1997), pp. 122ff.

13 *The Diary of John Grano*, p. 160.

14 *Ibid.*, p. 181.

15 *Ibid.*, p. 204.

16 *Ibid.*, p. 207.

17 *Ibid.*, p. 234.

18 *Ibid.*, p. 235.

19 Translation from Charlton and Hibberd, 'My father was a poor Parisian musician', 161–99.

20 *Anecdotes of George Frederick Handel and John Christopher Smith* (London, 1799), p. 6n.

21 Quoted in his autobiography published in Mattheson's *Grundlage einer Ehren-Pforte*, pp. 358ff.

22 See Ian Payne, 'Double Measures', *The Musical Times*, Winter 1998, 44–5.

23 Hurley, 'Handel's Compositional Process'.

24 See Paul Brainard, 'Aria and Ritornello: New Aspects of the Comparison Handel/Bach', in Peter Williams (ed.), *Bach, Handel, Scarlatti: Tercentenary Essays* (Cambridge, 1985), p. 23.

25 *The Lover's Discourse*, pp. 3–4.

26 From Johann Mattheson, *Der vollkommene Capellmeister* (Hamburg, 1739), pp. 122–3; part II, Chapter 4, 'Concerning Melodic Invention'. Translation from George J. Buelow, 'Mattheson's Concept of "Moduli" as a Clue to Handel's Compositional Process', *Göttinger Händel-Beiträge* 3 (1987), 272–8, with the musical examples corrected.

27 Friedrich Chrysander, *G. F. Händel*, 2 vols. (Leipzig, 1858–67), vol. I, p. 350, a propos *Solomon*.

28 Review by W[alter] E[mery] of Gerald Abraham (ed.), *Handel: A Symposium*, *Music & Letters* 35 (2) (1954), 164.

29 For these concepts, which separate Handel from his German – and indeed most other European – contemporaries, see John Armstrong, *The Secret Power of Beauty* (London, 2004).

30 Horace Walpole, *On Modern Gardening*, in *Anecdotes of painting in England*, vol. 4 (London, 1782), p. 308.

31 Anthony Hicks, private communication.

32 Jonathan Swift, *The Battel fought … between the Antient and the Modern Books* (London, 1704), p. 248.


## The *Concerti a due cori*

1 Letter to the Earl of Shaftesbury, 28 July 1743.

2 See *inter alia* Adrian Gilbert, *The New Jerusalem* (London, 2002).

3 See Burrows, *The Cambridge Companion to Handel*, p. 207.

4 See Stanley Sadie, *Handel Concertos* (BBC Publications, 1972), p. 64.

5 Many self-borrowings for the *Concerti a due cori* were first listed by Chrysander in *Händels Instrumentalkompositionen für grosses Orchester*, *Vierteljahrsschrift für Musikwissenschaft* 3 (1887), 182–8.

6 The 'Larghetto' in the tempo marking may have been added by J. C. Smith.

7 See Alfred Mann, *Handel: The Orchestral Music* (New York, 1996), pp. 136–7.

8 Samuel Butler, 'On "And the Glory of the Lord"' from *The Notebooks of Samuel Butler*, ed. Henry Festing Jones (London, 1912), p. 116. Butler probably did not understand the Italianate principles of elision, which would make 'glo–ryof' into two syllables.

9 See facsimile of the 1743 wordbook (Boston, 1995), p. 11.


## Politics and peace

1 See James Bohun, 'The Royal Fireworks and the Politics of Music in mid-Hanoverian England' (Ph.D. thesis, University of Alberta, 1993), pp. 77–8.

2 *Ibid.*, pp. 86–91.

3 See Miles Ogborn, *Spaces of Modernity: London's Geographies, 1680–1780* (Greenwich, NY, 1998), pp. 236–8.

4 See D. Burrows, 'Handel's Peace Anthem', *The Musical Times*, 1973, 1230.

5 For a survey with many illustrations, see Owen William Schaub, 'Pleasure Fires: Fireworks in the Court Festivals in Italy, Germany and Austria during the Baroque' (Ph.D. thesis, Kent State University, 1978).

6 *The Gentleman's Magazine*, April 1749, p. 186.

7 See Ursula Kirkendale, 'The Ruspoli Documents on Handel', *JAMS* 20 (1967), 222–73.

8 Mrs Boscawen, letter to Admiral Boscawen who, with General Amherst, retook Louisbourg for the English in 1758; he was brother-in-law to Charles Frederick.

9 See Sheila O'Connell, *London 1753* (London, 2003), p. 223 and Simon, *Handel*, p. 117.

10 See David M. Powers, 'The "Pastorale Héroïque": Origins and Development of a Genre' (Ph.D. thesis, University of Chicago, 1988).

11 A very similar March, arranged for keyboard in C major, is found in NYPL Drexel 5609, p. 210, in the context of Purcellian dance movements, suggesting that this canonic theme had been in circulation since at least the beginning of the century.

12 Reported in *Daily Advertiser* 18 April, *Penny London Post* 19 April and *Whitehall Evening Post* 20 April.

13 See David Hunter, 'Rode the 12,000? Counting Coaches, People, and Errors en Route to the Rehearsal of Handel's Music for the Royal Fireworks', a paper delivered at the Eleventh Biennial Conference on Baroque Music, Manchester, July 2004.

14 Information from David Hunter.

15 Public Record Office, WO 47/34, Minutes dated 19 April 1749: 'By the Surveyor General Ordered That Lieutenant Colonel Deal Master Gunner at St. James's send Eighteen Chambers with Two Rounds of Powder for each to Vaux Hall tomorrow Morning, the same to be delivered to Charles Frederick Esqr. or his Order, taking his Receipt to return them, and that a Proportion be drawn Accordingly' (information from Jacob Simon and David Hunter). 'Chambers' were small pieces of ordnance without a carriage, used to fire salutes.

16 The bracketed information was added in *The Gentleman's Magazine*'s account after the event; earlier, 7 o'clock had been quoted as the starting time.

17 See Joy Hancox, *The Queen's Chameleon: The Life of John Byrom – A Study of Conflicting Loyalties* (London, 1994).

18 [John Byrom], *Selections from the Journals and Papers of John Byrom, Poet, Diarist, Shorthand Writer, 1691–1763*, ed. Henri Talon (London, 1950), pp. 257ff. 'Peace without a vowel' is a mysterious expression, possibly mistranscribed (the original letter no longer survives). Could the reference be to the Latin abbreviation PX for PAX, or a reference to his shorthand system where vowels are represented by a dot?

19 Letter from Jemima, Marchioness Grey (1722–97) to Lady Mary Gregory (née Grey, 1719–61), the wife of Dr David Gregory, Professor of History and Modern Languages at Oxford, and Dean of Christ Church from 1756 (Bedfordshire and Luton Archives and Records Service, Wrest Park (Lucas) Collection; L30/9a/2). Transcription courtesy of David Hunter. See David Hunter, 'The Great Pretender', *The Musical Times*, Winter 2003, 41.

20 Letter to Horace Mann, 3 May 1749, *Horace Walpole's Correspondence*, ed. W. S. Lewis (New Haven, 1960), vol. XX, pp. 47–8.

## Music for the Royal Fireworks

1 From 'Causerie on Handel in England', an essay written to be read to a society of musicians in France, in a translation by August Hamon. Shaw sanctioned publication in the American *Ainslee's Magazine*, May 1913, and an unauthorised reprint, called "Bernard Shaw on Handel", appeared in *The Boston Evening Transcript*, 21 June 1913. The typescript, with alterations by Shaw, is in the Foundling Museum, Gerald Coke Handel Collection, shelf-mark HC 778. The French translation appeared in *Revue musicale S. I. M.*, 15 April 1913.

2 The quotation comes from Pope's explanatory footnote to the poem, p. 160.

3 See documentation in the Fitzwilliam Museum, Cfm Music MS 259, p. 79.

4 Under 'Le Tambour' in *Grand traité d'instrumentation et d'orchestration modernes*, op. 10 (Paris, 1843), Berlioz wrote: 'Leur effet est d'autant meilleur et s'ennoblit d'autant plus qu'ils sont en plus grand nombre; un seul tambour, surtout quand il figure au milieu d'un orchestre, m'a toujours paru mesquin et vulgaire.' Conductors take note!

5 D. F. Tovey, 'Handel. "Israel in Egypt"', in *Essays in Musical Analysis* 5 (Oxford, 1937), p. 85.

6 Philidor MS, 1705 Paris, Bibliothèque nationale, Rés.F.671.

7 See Burrows, 'Handel's Peace Anthem', 1230–2.

8 See Roberts, 'Handel's Borrowings from Telemann', 151.

9 'Drum ad libitum the second time drum warbling' is called for in 'See the conquering hero' (*Joshua*), presumably a Handelian mistake from the German 'Wirbel', a roll.

## Handel in other hands

1 *Letters of Felix Mendelssohn Bartholdy, from 1833 to 1847*, ed. Paul Mendelssohn Bartholdy and Carl Mendelssohn Bartholdy, trans. Lady Grace Wallace (London, 1863), pp. 386ff.

2 University of London Library, Williamson Partbooks, MS. 944/2/1–3; see Peter Holman, 'A New Source of Bass Viol Music from Eighteenth-Century England', *Early Music* 30 (1) (2003), 81–99.

3 See Jennifer Thorp, 'In Defence of Danced Minuets', *Early Music* 30 (1) (2003), 102.

4 Harty's *Suite from the Water Music* was published by Murdoch in 1922; in concert it was called 'The Royal Water Music' until 1934.

5 See C. G. Arnold, C. S. B., *The Orchestra on Record, 1896–1926: An Encyclopedia of Orchestral Recordings Made by the Acoustical Process* (Westport, Conn., 1997), p. 179.

6 Sleeve-note by Edward Johnson.

7 *Serse* was performed at the King's Theatre, not Covent Garden.

8 From John Huntley, *British Film Music* (London, [1947]), pp. 64–5.

9 Recorded in 1959 with Philomusica of London, Decca L'Oiseau-Lyre OL 50178.

10 DGG Archiv-Produktion LP (13012 AP).

11 Pye CML 33005, later re-issued as Pye Collector GSGC 14003/GGC 4003.

12 DGG Archiv-Produktion 427 2052 and 198 365.

13 Victor 12–0947 (12-inch 78rpm disc), Victor WDM-131 (7-inch 45rpm disc) and Victor LM-1165 (12-inch $33\frac{1}{3}$rpm disc).

## Performance parameters

1 Samuel Butler, *The Notebooks of Samuel Butler*, ed. Henry Festing Jones (London, 1912), p. 130.

2 Bruce Haynes, *A History of Performing Pitch* (Oxford, 2002) gives details of English pitch variations, which point to Sammartini being one of Handel's principal players.

3 Beecham's Handel arrangements included *The Gods Go A-Begging* (or *Les Dieux Mendiants*, written for Diaghilev in 1928), *The Origin of Design* (1932), *The Faithful Shepherd* (1941), *Amaryllis* (1943) and *The Great Elopement* (1945, re-titled *Love in Bath* in 1954).

# Select bibliography

## Pre-1800

Burney, Charles, *An Account of the Musical Performances in Westminster Abbey and the Pantheon ... In Commemoration of Handel* (London, 1785), facsimile reprint with an introduction by Peter Kivy (New York, 1979)

Coxe, William [son-in-law of J. C. Smith], *Anecdotes of George Frederick Handel and John Christopher Smith* (London, 1799), facsimile reprint with an introduction by Percy M. Young (New York, 1979)

[Mainwaring, John], *Memoirs of the Life of the Late George Frederic Handel* (London, 1760), facsimile reprint (Buren, 1964 and 1975); trans. Johann Mattheson, with commentary, as *Georg Friederich Händels Lebensbeschreibung* (Hamburg, 1761), reprint (Zurich, 1947)

Mattheson, Johann, *Critica Musica* (Hamburg, 1722)

   *Der vollkommene Capellmeister* (Hamburg, 1739)

   *Grundlage einer Ehren-Pforte* (Hamburg, 1740)

Price, Uvedale, *Essays on the Picturesque as compared with the Sublime and the Beautiful* (Hereford, 1798)

[Anon.], *A description of the machine for the fireworks, with all its ornaments, and a detail of the manner in which they are to be exhibited in St. James's Park, Thursday, April 27, 1749, on account of the general peace, signed at Aix La Chappelle ...* (London, 1749) (quarto pamphlet, 16 pp., published before the event)

[Anon.], *A Description of the Machine for the Fireworks, with all its ornaments: and a Detail of the manner in which they were exhibited in* St. James's Park *on Thursday the 27th of April, 1749, on Account of the General Peace, signed at* Aix La Chappelle ... (London, 1749) (octavo pamphlet, 8 pp., published after the event)

*A view of the public fire-works to be exhibited on occasion of the general peace, conducted at Aix-la-Chapelle, October 7, 1748 ... Engraved ... for the* LONDON MAGAZINE (London, 1748)

# Music in facsimile

*The Celebrated Water Musick in Seven Parts, viz. Two French Horns, Two Violins or Hoboys a Tenor and a Thorough Bass for the Harpsicord or Bass Violin Compos'd by Mr Handel* ... (London: Walsh, *c.* 1733) = *Walsh PP* (Performers Facsimiles; New York, [1990])

*Handel's Celebrated Water Musick Compleat. Set for the Harpsicord. To which is added, Two favourite Minuets, with Variations for the Harpsicord, By Geminiani* (London: Walsh, 1743) = *Walsh Hpd* (Performers Facsimiles; New York, [1985])

*Handel's water music adapted for the harpsicord or organ* (London: Longman, *c.* 1769) (Utrecht, 1995)

*Feuerwerksmusik – The Musick for the Royal Fireworks (Facsimile of the Autograph in the British Library)*, introd. Christopher Hogwood (Documenta Musicologica. Zweite Reihe: Handschriften-Faksimiles XXXII, Bärenreiter-Verlag, Kassel, 2004)

# Post-1800

Abraham, Gerald (ed.), *Handel: A Symposium* (London, 1954)

Best, Terence (ed.), *Handel Collections and their History* (Oxford, 1993)

Bohun, James, 'The Royal Fireworks and the Politics of Music in mid-Hanoverian England' (Ph.D. thesis, University of Alberta, 1993)

Burrows, Donald, 'Handel and Hanover', in Peter Williams (ed.), *Bach, Handel, Scarlatti. Tercentenary Essays* (Cambridge, 1985), 35–59

'The Christ Church *Water Music* Chamber Suite: Is It an Authentic Handelian Arrangement?', *Händel-Jahrbuch* 1993, 24–41

*Handel* (London, 2000)

Burrows, Donald and Martha Ronish, *A Catalogue of Handel's Musical Autographs* (Oxford, 1994)

Burrows, Donald and Robert D. Hume, 'George I, the Haymarket Opera Company and Handel's *Water Music*', *Early Music* 19 (3) (1991), 323–41

Burrows, Donald (ed.), *The Cambridge Companion to Handel* (Cambridge, 1997)

Butler, Samuel, *The Notebooks of Samuel Butler*, ed. Henry Festing Jones (London, 1912)

Byrom, John, *The private journal and literary remains*, vol. II, pt. 2 [1742–63], (Manchester, 1857)

Chrysander, Friedrich, 'Händels Instrumentalkompositionen für grosses Orchester', *Vierteljahrsschrift für Musikwissenschaft* 3 (1887), 182–8

Daub, Peggy Ellen, 'Music at the Court of George II' (Ph.D. thesis, Cornell University, 1985)

Dean, Winton, and John Merrill Knapp, *Handel's Operas 1704–1726*, revised edition (Oxford, 1994)

Deutsch, Otto Erich, *Handel: A Documentary Biography* (London, reprinted New York, 1974)

[Grano, John], *Handel's Trumpeter. The Diary of John Grano*, ed. John Ginger (New York, 1998)

Hancox, Joy, *The Queen's Chameleon: The Life of John Byrom – A Study of Conflicting Loyalties* (London, 1994)

Hill, Cecil, 'Die Abschrift von Händel's *Wassermusik* in der Sammlung Newman Flower', *Händel-Jahrbuch* 1971, 75–89

Hogwood, Christopher and Richard Luckett (eds.), *Music in Eighteenth-Century England: Essays In Memory of Charles Cudworth* (Cambridge, 1983)

Hudson, Frederick, 'Das "Concerto" in *Judas Maccabeus* indentifiziert', *Händel-Jahrbuch* 1974, 119–33

Huntley, John, *British Film Music* (London, [1947])

Hurley, David Ross, *Handel's Muse: Patterns of Creation in his Oratorios and Musical Dramas, 1743–1751* (Oxford, 2001)

Larsen, Jens Peter, *Handel's Messiah: Origins, Composition, Sources* (London, 1957)

Mann, Alfred, *Handel: the Orchestral Music* (New York, 1996)

Marx, Hans Joachim, 'Händel's *Concerti a due cori* (HWV 332–334) und ihre kompositionsgeschichtlichen Grundlagen', *Händel-Jahrbuch* 1996/7, 85–98

O'Connell, Sheila, *London 1753* (London, 2003)

Ogborn, Miles, *Spaces of Modernity: London's Geographies, 1680–1780* (Greenwich, NY, 1998)

Powers, David M., 'The "Pastorale Héroïque": Origins and Development of a Genre' (Ph.D. thesis, University of Chicago, 1988)

Redlich, Hans, 'Georg Friedrich Händel und seine Verleger', in *Musik und Verlag* (Kassel, 1968), 493–501

Roberts, John (ed.), *Handel Sources Series: Materials for the Study of Handel's Borrowing*, 9 vols. (New York and London, 1986)

Robinson, Percy, *Handel and His Orbit* (London, 1908), reprinted with new introduction by Jens Peter Larsen (Da Capo Press, 1979)

Sadie, Stanley, *Handel Concertos* (London, 1972)

Sayle, R. T. D., *The Barges of the Merchant Taylors' Company*, printed for private circulation, 1933

Schaub, Owen William, 'Pleasure Fires: Fireworks in the Court Festivals in Italy, Germany and Austria during the Baroque' (Ph.D. thesis, Kent State University, 1978)

Serwer, Howard, 'The World of the *Water Music*', *Händel-Jahrbuch* 1996/7, 101–11

Simon, Jacob (ed.), *Handel: A Celebration of his Life and Times* (London, 1985)

Smith, William C., *Handel: A Descriptive Catalogue of the Early Editions* (Oxford, 1960, 2nd edn 1970)

    *Concerning Handel, His Life and Works: Essays* (London, 1948, facsimile reprint by Hyperion Press, 1979)

Taylor, Sedley, *The Indebtedness of Handel to Works by Other Composers: A Presentation of Evidence* (Cambridge, 1906)

Warren, Ray, 'Orchestral Music', in *Hamilton Harty, His Life and Music* (Belfast, [1978])

Winemiller, John T., 'Handel's Borrowing and Swift's Bee: Handel's "Curious" Practice and the Theory of Transformative Imitation' (Ph.D. thesis, University of Chicago, 1994)

Wolff, Hellmuth Christian, *Die Barockoper in Hamburg (1678–1738)* (Wolfenbüttel, 1957)

# Index